MOUNTAINS ACCORDING TO G

Also by Geraint Thomas with Tom Fordyce

The World of Cycling According to G
The Tour According to G

MOUNTAINS
ACCORDING
TO G

GERAINT THOMAS

Written with Tom Fordyce

Quercus

First published in Great Britain in 2020 by Quercus.

Quercus Editions Ltd
Carmelite House
50 Victoria Embankment
London EC4Y 0DZ

An Hachette UK company

A CIP catalogue record for this book is available
from the British Library

HB ISBN 978 1 52941 096 9
Ebook ISBN 978 1 52941 097 6

Print   p.A.

Papers used by   nsible sources.

For Macsen, my greatest adventure to date.

Riding these climbs is a lot easier than some of the long nights we've had together, but I wouldn't change a thing. Maybe we'll ride them together one day, or maybe I'll just bore you with stories about them. But let's definitely ski down Alpe d'Huez.

I Macsen,

Fy antur fwyaf hyd yn hyn.

Mae reidio'r dringfeydd hyn dipyn yn haws na rhai o'r nosweithiau hir ry'n ni wedi'u cael gyda'n gilydd ond byddwn i'n newid dim byd. Efallai y cawn ni eu reidio nhw gyda'n gilydd ryw ddydd neu efallai y gwna i dy ddiflasu di gyda straeon amdanyn nhw yn lle. Ond yn bendant, gad i ni sgïo lawr Alpe d'Huez gyda'n gilydd.

Contents

Introduction

Mountains are special. You ride your bike, you want to ride up mountains. Maybe to race, maybe to train, but always to get to the top – to prove that you can do it, to take on the tarmac and the elements and the fear and beat them all.

That's why we climb on our bikes. For the challenge, for the satisfaction. For the views, for the stories afterwards. To share the experience of our heroes, to maybe write a few epics ourselves.

Mountains are where the biggest races are won and lost. They're where the atmosphere is best, where the fans can watch for free and see more of the riders than anywhere else. They're where the Tour and the Giro and the Vuelta are decided, where names are made and where men and women can break. Because they're scary, too, climbs. It can feel impossible getting up them and crazy getting down. You experience heat so intense you're tipping bidons of water over your head. You can get hail and snow so heavy that you lose all sensation in your fingers and feet. You see valleys below and peaks up ahead. You feel the wind and see the drops and you feel more alive than anywhere else on your bike.

But all that makes them hard is also what makes them so appealing. The tougher they are, the longer the memories last. The more riders' names ring out: Anquetil, Merckx, Induráin. You cannot hide on a mountain, and the truth they bring is inescapable. You can't bodge it on a big climb. It's you and the road and what you have in your heart and your legs. They're pain and they're magic. They punish you but they reward you with so much, too.

You can love football and never get the chance to score a goal at Wembley. You can love rugby and never get the chance to dive over the try line at the Principality Stadium, or watch tennis all your life yet only dream of making a volley at the net on Centre Court at Wimbledon. But in cycling you can ride exactly the same climbs as those legends. You can experience exactly what they went through. You can ride up Alpe d'Huez and the Koppenberg and everything in between.

And so this is my book about them. How I get up them, what they do to us in the pro peloton. How *you* can get up them, where the attacks come, where the danger lurks. What we eat and drink, the mental privations we go through as well as the physical. The great days I've enjoyed, the horrors I've gone through, too. The secret data, the secret names, the reason they stay with us long after we've returned to the flat and the prosaic.

It's a personal list. It's the ones that have mattered to me as a child, a junior aiming high and a pro racing higher. They're spread across the world and they range from the small and lumpy to the big and brutal. But they're all special, and they're all magical. And they're all out there, free to ride and waiting for you to have a go.

Enjoy, and suffer, and enjoy a bit more. My mountains are your mountains. Let's climb.

UK

Rhigos

An insider tip to start us off: the proper Valleys pronunciation of Rhigos is not the 'Regoss' that you might hear in the cosmopolitan coastal areas of Wales, but 'Rick-oss'. And the Valleys has naming rights, so that's how I'd like it in your head for the duration of this climb.

Rhigos has clout in south Wales. This and the Bwlch, over towards Bridgend, are your rites of passage. The Tumble? That comes later. You cut your teeth on Rhigos. You make your name on the Bwlch. You establish it on the Tumble.

And so I knew about it, and what it meant, when I was on one of my first Sunday morning runs with the Maindy Flyers Club, fourteen years old. I just wasn't expecting to see it. I'd never been so far on a bike, and had already experienced a feeling of intense panic when I'd recognized the Storey Arms outward bounds centre, which in my experience was a long coach ride away from my school in Cardiff. To have gone that far on a bike was both something to be proud of and a potential disaster. I was so far from home that there was no way I could be dropped and still hope to survive. All that, and then the realization that I'd have to summit Rhigos to have any hope of seeing Cardiff or my family ever again.

It was never easy then. The first time I attempted it without adult supervision was in a small escape with a couple of mates, riding out to watch the big boys in the Five Valleys race – one of the highlights of the British cycling calendar, part of a national series which went all over the UK. One of the toughest and most attractive of races, taking in all the major climbs South Wales can throw at you, an annual highlight for those of us in love with road racing and hills.

We rode out to the biggest climbs to watch the race, Tour de France style. A beautiful day, blue skies, sun shining, not enough water or sunscreen. And so we were wasted by the time the Rhigos and Bwlch had finished with us, and we still had the recurring issue of getting back to Cardiff afterwards. In what was to prove a precursor to my early days with the pro ranks, I suffered enormously, but blew up slightly later than one of the other lads, so was able to recount the tale later with my morale high. It's amazing how good finishing not-quite-last can feel.

And because of the way that cycling obsessions can work, I found myself racing Five Valleys a few years later as a pale junior. We were due to approach Rhigos from the Hirwaun side, to the north. As an eighteen-year-old, the goal was just to survive. Our coach, Darren Tudor, was realistic: lads, get to 100 miles. That'll get you to the finishing circuit in Port Talbot. Do that and you've had a good day.

The nerves were clanging, partly because it was Rhigos,

partly because it was Five Valleys, partly because of the riders I found myself going up Rhigos in Five Valleys with. There were the local tough guys of the Welsh scene, guys you rode with only on rare occasions. Small men with sinewy legs and an ability to suffer in silence. 'Jeez, he's turned up for the club run today! This is going to be tough. Glad I had that extra round of toast this morning . . .'

There were younger under-twenty-three riders who were being talked up on the British scene, like Dan Fleeman. And there was Magnus Bäckstedt, an actual stage winner at the Tour de France, shortly to triumph at Paris-Roubaix, which would really have done for me. And yet going up Rhigos, I was in the lead group with all these men. Not leading the lead group – I was eighteen, I was on restricted gears, I was only meant to be getting to Port Talbot – but sitting third or fourth wheel, hanging on, living the dream.

There's a long final hairpin on Rhigos, of which more shortly. But as we swung round it, I glanced down to my left and saw Bäckstedt – actual Magnus Bäckstedt, elite pro rider, Swedish superstar, clever enough to marry a Welsh girl – 15 metres back.

Whoah. This, I thought to myself, is now unbelievable. This is too good. Forget the bright lights of Port Talbot, its quaint, picturesque charms. Nothing else that happens today can ever top this. Even as we went over the top of the climb and began the descent, and I realized that with my restricted gears I would have to pedal my nuts off to keep any of my glorious gains in hand – even as I tried to find the slipstream of a bigger man, or an actual man – I knew that Rhigos had a place in my heart for ever.

The details. There are two ways you can climb Rhigos, the more customary being from that same Hirwaun side, out of the village on the A4059 and then the A4061. You'll be climbing for about six kilometres, the gradient averaging just over 5% and never ramping up beyond 7%. That's a decent gauntlet to have thrown down but not quite a slap in the face. You and Rhigos can get along.

The usual run-in takes you over Penderyn Moor, dropping down into the village, past the distillery. Now is not the time for fine Welsh single malts, but perhaps consider it for a treat when your day in the saddle is done.

You'll come through an industrial estate. You'll see the old mines, the valleys that they nurtured, a very Welsh vista for a very Welsh climb. You turn left off the roundabout and then it's on you – a long, straight drag, a grind while seated in the saddle, open to the winds that come in from the west. Sometimes they manifest themselves as a crosswind, which is awkward. More often they're a headwind, which, when you're going uphill, is just plain unfair.

That's the first third of your climb. Gritting your teeth, getting it done. Gradually, you'll see the road start curving round to the left, and up to your right you can see the road switching back right, another long drag and then a long hairpin back to your left. The road snakes across your eyeline, and being able to see everything that lies in wait can come as a blow. Especially if you're fourteen, you're already nailed and the headwind is bringing a load of snow with it too.

When the trees start the gradient kicks up but it's easier to ride – out of the wind, more all around to distract you, rather than a road going on and on in front of you. You can see tracks off through the pines and grass to your right, trails where the Welsh Rally used to race every October, and it's hard not to dream of being in a car, a gentle press with the sole of the right foot accelerating you up these slopes rather than the endless pedalling and all that road still to go.

Back round to the right, and it begins to flatten off. You might find yourself wondering where the actual top is, because it's so open now, so here's the second key insider tip: look for the ice-cream van that's always parked up in the lay-by on your right. It's saved me a few times, that van – a cheeky can of Coke to stuff in my back pocket if I'm out of energy, the occasional ice cream if it's after the season's ended and I'm allowed to be Normal Geraint rather than No You Don't Geraint.

My mate Andy Hoskins once tried to hand us up some ice creams there during Five Valleys, a lovely if misguided thought. But logic doesn't have much place on Rhigos. It was coming down there as a kid, broken, where we stopped at a shop in Treochy to buy us the sugary drinks we needed to get home, only for my mate to blow our entire £3 on diet lemonade. It was after going down the other side and another day where we stopped in the petrol station in Hirwaun and ended up buying microwave burgers. We used to ride out there and back from Cardiff when I was in the sixth form at school, returning in the dark with one rear light between us. We'd go over it, descend, turn around, climb back up, descend and then do it all again. We lost our minds on Rhigos, in a beautiful way.

It's probably twenty minutes of effort for a good club rider, maybe twelve or thirteen for me if I'm in shape. I tend not to ride it flat out as it's usually a nostalgic trip out for me when I'm back in Cardiff in November or December, and with time I've also found myself favouring the ride up from the other side, the Treorchy road. I'm aware this is slightly sacrilegious, but for a place called Treorchy it has an unexpectedly European feel: a busy little town, the climb ramping up straight off the high street, a couple of long hairpins and some first-class tarmac up through the trees.

When you race in France, you become accustomed to fighting for a good position coming through a town or village at the foot of the climb, diving through a few narrow, twisty corners, jumping out of your saddle to stay with the initial acceleration as you leave the buildings behind and head into the woods. This is the Treorchy vibe, and it's steeper and angrier than the Hirwaun side but far less bleak and with much more to distract you, so it works. There's even a mystery halfway up, a little white house so small it looks like it was built for a Borrower – almost like a weird shrine. There were often flowers left outside, the occasional wreath, as if someone met a cruel end here. It puzzled me for so long that I had to look it up in the end: turns out it was a watchman's hut, used by a lovely old boy who used to clear the road of sheep and rocks for the council, and who made little sculptures from old plastic and copper wire to add a touch of colour to the landscape.

And by the time you've mulled that over – the scene, the number of bouquets, the backstory – you've banged out another kilometre, and all is good in the world. That doesn't happen on the Hirwaun side. A third of the way up you leave the oak trees behind. For a few sweet fleeting moments, you can fool yourself into thinking you can see the top, but it's a cruel optical illusion. You look back down into the valley and you can see the dark slate roofs of the houses you came through a few minutes ago, and it all feels a little like a Welsh version of the Col du Portet in the Pyrenees: rock face on your right, fresh air to your left, a long view out over the valley if you're dawdling and losing your climbing focus.

When the weather's good, it's a joy up the top of Rhigos. Since it's in south Wales, I'm used to it not being so nice. Riding it as a junior one morning with three mates, coming up from the Hirwaun side, the weather was terrible. Rain coming in sideways, hitting us directly in the face – but we were young and keen, thinking: this is what it's like in the pro peloton when the weather is bad; this is great.

And it was, until we hit the descent and Rob punctured. Nobody bothered to help him. It was too cold. Instead we huddled together behind a rock trying to hide from the elements, leaving him to sort it himself. Not that we could have helped too much, even if we had tried. None of us had any feeling in our hands, let alone the strength to pull off a tyre. Instead we shouted abuse from behind our rock, which is the sort of thing boys do to their mates. When I then punctured in Treorchy, Rob actually helped me fix mine. Which is not the sort of thing boys usually do for their mates.

You get a good sweat on when you're climbing Rhigos hard, but you never slip too many layers off, because the odds on it raining at the top are high. It's not one to linger on for the same reasons. Having an ice cream? You may well savour the top bit and then smash down the lower half as the cold kicks in. Reaching for the emergency can of Coke? You're likely to slightly rush it and spend the next twenty minutes burping gently like your grandad after a few too many pints down the local.

There's a term in the peloton for a rider considered strong but quite thick: Domestos. I'd describe the Hirwaun side of Rhigos in similar terms. He's not the most fun character most of the time, and time in his company can drag, conversation something of a grind. When you get to know him a little more, though, he becomes friendlier, and you appreciate his charms. But you still prefer his brother over the other side in Treorchy – a hard man, too, but with much more to say. Treorchy is the guy you hear at the bar as you walk into the pub, throwing a few stories out, giving you a slap on the back that's quite stiff but meant well. Meanwhile, Hirwaun is sitting by himself in the corner, drinking pints of old man's ale.

That's Rhigos.

When you turn pro, you tend to have a checklist in your head of all the great races you want to ride before you're back down to civilian ranks. The Tour de France, of course. The other two Grand Tours, at least once. The Monuments, one after another. Flanders and Paris-Roubaix, before the others.

It's the same as an amateur rider in south Wales. You have to tick off Rhigos, then the Bwlch, then the Tumble. Any club you join will first tell you its tales and then take you up it to make your own. Which makes it such a disgrace that my father-in-law has yet to take it on. He's happy to give me grief for not being the purest of pure climbers, but now he's riding himself – albeit only in the fairest of weather – he's still riding scared of Rhigos. And, as a result, cannot yet consider himself a proper rider. His choice, his outcome.

The Tumble

There's something about the Tumble that gets to you. Before you've even ridden it, you've heard the stories. You've heard the myths. The old boys in your cycling club – they'll whisper about it to you young ones. Boys, it's brutal. Toughest climb in south Wales, this one. You'll find nothing longer and nothing steeper, lads.

You know about it, but it's mysterious, too. Rhigos – that's much closer to home, if you've grown up in Cardiff or along the coast. It's familiar from early on. The Tumble is much further on – deeper into the countryside, a much longer ride, a destination rather than something you could do on the way to somewhere else. The Tumble? It's out there. Waiting.

It's got history, the Tumble. And it wasn't even always the Tumble. Back in the old days it was known as the Keepers. It was only when the Kellogg's Tour of Britain started going up it in the mid-1980s that the race organizers looked at it on an Ordnance Survey map and saw the word 'Tumble' halfway up it that it was reborn. There used to be a Tumble Inn there. Maybe that's where the name came from. But because the Tumble Inn tumbled down a long time ago, there's no regulars to ask. Just the myths.

So. The raw details. It's 512 metres up at the top. It's about five kilometres in length, depending where exactly you measure the start from. And it drags – an average gradient of just over 8%, ramps of up to 13%, very little respite at all.

Those numbers are why the Grand Prix of Wales used it from about 1987 onwards and the junior Tour of Wales loves using it as the set-piece finishing climb on the final day of the race. As a junior back then, that was one of the best races you could hope to do. It was the one that made you feel most like being a proper pro rider in one of the Grand Tours. Lots of individual stages, days where different types of young riders could shine – the big units, the sprinters; the power boys, the ones who would have made good centres down at the local rugby club; the in-betweeners, who could hang on to both; and then the skinny ones, the mountain goats who would wait and wait for the grand finale up the Tumble on the Bank Holiday Monday. We'd be talking about it all week. The local club warriors – in our heads like pros who just happened to have day jobs – would be peppered with questions. The experts would be sought out and held in the highest regard. 'Oh, you know Pete?' 'What, old Pete?' 'Yeah. Went up the Tumble yesterday.' 'No way! He's mental!'

It starts by the village of Govilon, just out to the west of Abergavenny, in Monmouthshire. If you're asking for directions, pronounce it 'G'vylon', rather than 'Govvy-lon', or else the locals might send you somewhere far away. And then it's a technical run-in, from that direction, with a few too many speed bumps to be entirely happy if you're on a bike, especially in a frantic peloton racing to the start of the climb. It narrows in sections as well. Through the stone arch of a railway bridge, left turn and a kick over a little humpback bridge.

No matter how many times you ride it, it always seems to start from nowhere. One moment you're on the flat of the B4246, the next you swing round a left-hand corner and you're going up. There's a big hedge on the left, a white house on your right, and boom – you're up and going, the road black and menacing in front of you at close to 10% already.

Your positioning in the peloton or little group doesn't matter too much at this stage – there's so much climbing ahead of you – but you shouldn't let yourself drift too far back, because the further back you go the more little accelerations you'll have to make to hold your position, or you'll drift back even further. Neither could you then choose your line around the first real corner, a tight right hairpin. You want to go round the outside line here, rather than hugging the inside. It's too steep the shorter way and takes too much out of you. You might save a few metres, but it'll take it back from you. Stay on the left side of the carriageway, trust your tactics, trust your knowledge of what lies ahead. Too far back and you've no choice. You'll be sprinting to regain contact, and no one wants to be sprinting at this point on the Tumble.

Now it's the trees. The road surface is getting worse, lumpier and slower, and if it's the wrong time of year, the dead leaves under your wheels can make it slipperier and nastier. For the first time you don't really feel like you're in south Wales. It's not just the steepness and it's not just the length. It's the forested hillside, in an area where the lumps are more gradual and usually quite bare. That's the thing about the Tumble – it doesn't make sense, even where it sits. It's like Mont Ventoux in the way it just sticks up from its surroundings, an ominous presence in the foreground as you close in on it. You can't miss it. And so the whisper goes round the group again. 'Phwoar. There it is. There's the Tumble . . .'

Through the trees, then the cover gradually thinning out. It's the cattle grid around halfway that you're waiting for. It's still a grind from here, still a long way to go, and if you're racing, the last thing you want is to be blowing and have too little left for the slog and headwinds up ahead. This can even feel like the lowest point mentally, because of what has already been taken out of your legs and what is still to come. The gradient is going to get easier but the road surface is about to get stickier and heavier and now, if there's wind and there's rain, they'll both have you in their sights. No cover from trees, from hedges or rock formations on either side. Just that same sense you get on Ventoux when you pop out of the trees and on to the lunar landscape towards the top: right, be nice to me, there's nothing I can do if you want to turn bad.

There's no magic trick for the next few kilometres. You just have to get through them. They will come to an end, even if on bad days they feel like they never will. Wait for the first corner you can see up ahead. Anything that takes your attention away from the long road stretching away in front of you.

It's quite weird, up there. No trees, no vegetation except scrubby grass and damp, dark green moss. As it opens up even more you can look down to your right and see the valley below. Glance to your left and there's no great cliff wall, just that wet grass going up and away at a mind-numbing gradient. In winter it's a cruel place. There's always wind. It's just a question of how strong it is, how straight-on it wants to be, how much rain it's carrying with it. I've had days up there when the wind has done a deal with the rain to come in at exactly the right angle to get under the rim of your helmet and right into your face. Scouring you, freezing your nose, dripping down your chin and neck and trying to infiltrate your jersey and jacket.

It's never entirely dry up there either, even in the middle of summer. There is always a dampness in the air. The road doesn't look that wet – it's rare to see large puddles – but that's partly because it has such a heavy feel to it. I know very little about the ideal mix when trying to slap tarmac on an unfriendly mountain, but it feels like they added extra sand to the recipe for this one. It's the opposite of an Italian road, which is typically smooth, almost polished, and as effective at absorbing rain as a marble table. It could rain all day at the top of the Tumble and the road would just drink it all in. And it's rough, too – like they had such a nightmare getting it to set that they couldn't be bothered to bring the heavy roller on. It's a road that would be dreadful to crash on. It would rip you to shreds.

So it's horrible. But it's always rideable. This is not a climb that should force you off your bike. And it's a beauty, in its own way. The top of it is so different in character to a normal, humdrum environment that it leaves a mark on you every time. There are hills you ride up and instantly forget about. You never forget the Tumble. You never wake up the next morning and think, what was it I did yesterday?

I said there are no magic tricks. There is something you can do, something that kept me going through the three consecutive days of 12-hour rides I did for the NHS during the Coronavirus outbreak in early 2020. You break it all down. You don't think about what you have left, you think about what you've done already. Four kilometres to the top? Right. Just focus on this first kilometre. It's a thousand metres. It's probably a lot less than 500 pedal strokes. Look, in the time we've been talking you've done twenty. And that was without even noticing. You will get there.

Soon you'll see the top. And while you might not be there yet, you know now that the pain is almost over. It has a proper top, too, the Tumble. Rhigos – that plateaus. You can wonder if you've made it. On the Tumble there's no mistaking it. The cold blue of Keepers Pond on your left, a little junction on your left and you've made it.

Have a look around when you have. You'll feel the height. Have a listen, too. On the big Alpine climbs, it's the strange chirping and whistling of the marmots that accompanies you at the summits. On the Tumble, it's the bleat and baa of sheep. Luke Rowe once had a sketchy sheep-related moment just over the top, at the start of the descent, when a stray lamb bolted straight off the verge and under his bike. He was only thirteen at the time (Luke, that is – it's a rare sheep that makes it to its teens), and for a moment he feared the worst, only for the lamb to roll to safety, clouted by the big ring, but saved by the fact that Luke had just shifted his chain from the smaller ring with all the climbing done. No cyclist likes the idea of a high-speed crash, let alone one with an animal on a road surface as rough as sandpaper, so there was a giddy sense of relief as we careered down the other side with both man and beast still upright.

I feel slightly as if I have a debt to settle with the Tumble.

I've never had an amazing day when racing up it. When I was eighteen and riding the Tour of Wales, sitting in second overall, Dan Martin beat me up there. I've struggled to let that go. An Irishman from Birmingham beating a Welsh boy on the Tumble. It's angered me ever since.

We also used the top part during the time-trial at the Junior Tour, starting just outside Brynmawr and heading along the moor on the B4248 towards Blaenavon before turning sharp left on to the backside of the Tumble for a couple of kilometres to the top. My late aunt and uncle, Chris and Ade, would always support me by coming out to cheer me on here, and so when I ride it now, I ride it with warm memories of them, too.

I have ridden it the other way. Come up from Big Pit, do a monstrous there-and-back. Very few tend to do this because it's even harder and steeper, and if you want to start from the southern end, the ride into it is along busy, dangerous roads. The gradient you climb at the bottom near Govilon – it's that all the way up from the Big Pit side, after a more gradual ascent on the road from Pontypool. You can do it, but you won't do it often.

So it's all about the Govilon side for me. And if I had to compare the Tumble to a rugby player – which I should, bearing in mind we're in south Wales – I'd have to say that it was Alun Wyn Jones. It keeps going whatever happens. It's full-on from start to finish. The harder it gets, the more enjoyment it takes from it.

And it does not care what you think of it. It will throw everything at you, and you will not be able to escape. But here's the thing – the more time you spend with it, the more respect you have for it, and the more it drags out of you. You might not be sure if it likes you; it's such a long ride from Cardiff to get there that you'll be vulnerable every time you renew acquaintance, and you're never looking pretty at the top. But it's enjoyable, too, in its own brutal way. You don't ride your bike to have it easy. It's not snooker. It's not bowls. You want to be tested. And the Tumble will take great pride in pushing you all the way.

Cat and Fiddle

There are harder climbs in the north-west of England. Holme Moss is a brute. There are more spectacular ones; you don't forget Winnats Pass in a hurry, and the Goyt Valley road alongside the two reservoirs is a beauty. There are longer ones: take Snake Pass all the way across the Peaks and it stays in your legs. You go up to the Lakes and Whinlatter and Honister and Hardknott, and you can get hard and long and beautiful all in one go.

But the Cat and Fiddle matters, for where it is and what it does. If you ride your bike around there – coming out of Manchester or Buxton or Stoke – you'll have tested yourself on its rough tarmac. It's a proper road, taking you from the west side of the Peaks in Macclesfield up to the top, before the descent into the limestone valleys and granite plateaus, and it's about motorbikes and big wagons as much as bikes. It's eleven kilometres of bends and efforts and views, if you're lucky, and it transports you from one world to another: from urban streets and supermarkets up to a bleak landscape of wind and rain and tufts of grass that squelch if you try to sit down on them for a rest.

In short, it's Arsenal under latter-period Arsène Wenger. It's not outstanding in any one category but it's always top four. The best will usually get past it, but sometimes it can hurt the best, too. You feel an affection for it even as you understand its limitations.

When I moved from south Wales to Manchester to ride with the GB academy under Rod Ellingworth, the Cat and Fiddle was our go-to climb, more so than the famous Brickworks one out of Pott Shrigley – the easiest to get to from the southern Manchester suburbs, a good stretch to knock out our training efforts, plenty of adventure thrown in, too. We'd always begin from the Macc side and we'd never ever stop off in the pub at the top which gives the climb its name, which in retrospect is a shame. I've passed it so many times that a loosener in the saloon bar feels overdue. It always looks like the loneliest pub in the world. There's no habitation for miles around. You don't look at your watch at 9pm and think, might just pop into the Cat and Fiddle for a cheeky half – not unless you're bivouacking on the blasted moor at the top.

There's no hiding from the weather when it comes at you on this climb. On a clear day you can see all the way north-west to Manchester, see the curves of the big white radio telescope at Jodrell Bank sticking up from the Cheshire plains. It's just there aren't that many clear days. It gets wild on the Cat and Fiddle.

The numbers don't quite do it justice. An average gradient of just over 3%, but with sections of up to 8%, and a stiff 6% for the first two kilometres out of town.

It's a solid, decent climb. Drop your speed too much and the wagons chugging up will blast you with their horns, for if they lose their momentum it takes them an age of huffing and puffing to get it back. There are average-speed cameras overhead to keep the motorbikers from opening up too much; a sign warning of low-flying aircraft, which makes you wonder if maybe they aren't a little too low if they're having to warn people in cars and on bikes.

Our training up it for the academy was track-specific. A riding position that was closer to the one we'd use on a time-trial bike, with hips rotated forward. Twenty seconds on, forty seconds off. Short and intense or going longer on bigger gears. I was always being told to shift up the block rather than down. I liked to grind. Grinding doesn't work for the track. You get strong but you lose some of that speed from your legs.

The Cat and Fiddle was the first place I did some proper structured efforts – from the 20/40s, to Zone 3s, to full-on bottom-to-top threshold efforts. It's where we learned, or at least started to learn, how to judge effort: where to push on, where to recover slightly. Before the Cat, I just trained as any junior did. Ride your bike as much as you can. Efforts? Nah – just go hard for however long the climb is. The Cat was where we learned our trade.

But it wasn't those efforts that hurt the most. It was what else the Cat brought home. There was a time one winter when snow began to fall as Ian Stannard and I made our way round the Tesco's roundabout in Maccles-field. A mile in it was settling on our arms and backs. Another mile on it was in our eyes. Five minutes later we could no longer see the road.

Each of us knew what the other was thinking: if this is bad, imagine what it's going to be like at the top. Shall we turn back? Shouldn't we have turned back already?

Of course, neither of us wanted to say it. Neither wanted to be the first to crack. So we kept going, fighting our way into what was now a blizzard, all the way to the pub. And then we looked at each other and gulped. If it was bad coming up, what was it going to be like going back down at 50 miles an hour?

We descended into Buxton, sitting on our top tubes rather than the saddle, one foot unclipped and dabbing down on the icy road in a desperate search for a little extra stability. The question was why we were heading into Buxton rather than back home. It was further away. The weather was getting even bleaker, if that was possible. The regrets were heavier by the frozen minute.

But it's been worse. A year or two later, I did the climb in pleasant meteorological conditions but with increasingly problematic intestinal ones. What had begun in Manchester as a strange looseness and developed by Macclesfield into a regular cramping had, by the top of the climb, become a mission-critical need to let it all go.

The pub was shut, not that they would have been

open to the idea of a man in tight-fitting clothes and noisy cleats legging it past the bar without ordering and shoulder-barging his way through the door to the gents. The landscape all around offered little in the way of cover beyond those ankle-high tufts of wet grass.

They're not proud moments, the aftermath of these incidents. There's relief but no pride. You look around and hope that a pair of walkers enjoying a hike through the hills are not frozen in open-mouthed horror a few metres away. You hope an inquisitive dog is not following its nose with its tongue out. You pull your shorts back up and pray you can make it home before calamity strikes again.

Punishment, in every way. I remember the night of the Champions League final of 2005, Liverpool against Milan in an absolute epic, and also the occasion of my birthday. You don't go out as a young cyclist, not really, but this seemed like the sort of double excuse that any coach would clear. My housemate Matt Brammeier agreed and decided to come to the pub with me. My other housemates, Ed Clancy and a certain Mark Cavendish, disagreed, and went to bed early.

I didn't think we stayed out that late. The game did go to extra time and penalties. We did stop off at Subway for emergency food on the way home. But all would have been okay had the greatest sprinter of his generation not turned snitch and dobbed us in to Rod and Dave Brailsford.

The next morning's bollocking was an epic of the genre. Banned from the big Five Valleys race that I'd been looking forward to so much; sent up the Cat and Fiddle with Steve Cummings and Brad Wiggins, who had just returned from riding the Giro and was thus in the sort of climbing form that takes a British hill and chomps it down as an hors d'oeuvre.

It wasn't slow, that day. It wasn't a short ride. Hanging on by my fingernails, wasting whatever spare breath I had asking Brad what it was really like to actually ride a Grand Tour, all the time thinking, I'm never going to take the Cat and Fiddle for granted ever again. And I'm never, ever going to forgive Cav.

Belgium

Oude Kwaremont

27/3/2015, winning E3 Harelbeke
Duration: 4 mins 40 secs
Distance: 2.21km
Ave speed: 28.2kph
Ave cadence: 82

If ever there was a climb that lies at the heart of cycling history, it's the Kwaremont. A cobbled climb in a land in love with the cobbled climb, a steep little monster in a country without great peaks, a section of stone and mud that has defined some of the greatest riders of all time.

It's about the races that slog up it – the Tour of Flanders, of course, but also the springtime races that precede it, like Omloop Het Nieuwsblad, E3 and Kuurne-Brussels-Kuurne – and it's about the muscular champions who have led up it; but it's also about everything that happens before you even get there. The race for the bottom of the Kwaremont is as important as the race on it.

The final time you approach the Kwaremont, you have to be in the top fifteen as you enter a sharp right-hander about a kilometre out from the climb or your race is over. It's that narrow and that hard to ride that it becomes that simple. The front is out of trouble. Anywhere else is in it. The guy in front of you loses the wheel of the guy in front of him? Done for. Now or never, right here. And so the run-in to what is the actual challenge becomes a race that on its own is one of the fiercest you find yourself in all season.

You're on a good three-lane road, three kilometres out, descending from a little rise. Nice, smooth tarmac, straightish, all hammering along in a constantly shifting pack at sixty kilometres an hour. Elbows out, shouting, swearing. Even the three lanes aren't enough to contain all the mad surges and moves being launched, and so there are riders on the hard shoulder and the bike path. It's crazy, but this is Belgium. Big concrete flowerpots sticking out into the road, guys hopping from pavement to road back to pavement, riders strung out across the road. Technically, you're not meant to be on the pavement, but that doesn't seem to stop people willing to take a punt on the commissaires not spotting them or focusing on the other bloke who's been doing it for a couple of seconds longer.

Sometimes you don't have a choice, as Luke Rowe once found out. A rider cutting across his line, forcing him to swerve right. Two options: on to the bike path, or into a concrete plant pot. He made the right decision for a rider and the wrong one for the commissaires. Race over.

At the end of this fast, crazy section, you dive into a

90-degree right-hander, in the top ten if you've ridden it well, and it instantly pinches in, except now you're less than a kilometre before the foot of the climb, so frantic doesn't even come close. Pavements come and go, gutters appearing and then snaking off, and there are riders bunny-hopping and taking crazy gambles down the outside to move up, even dodging in and out of spectators. I must be getting old. I used to be that guy. I used to be that risk-taker. Not any more.

All to get to the front. All to avoid being churned backwards when you thought you were already there. Except you find yourself at the front, and you don't actually want to be there too long, because then you're in the wind and working too hard before you've even begun to climb, and you're making it too easy for your rivals tucked on your rear wheel.

It may already be too late. I was riding Flanders when Niki Terpstra and Alexander Kristoff attacked after the Taaienberg, around six or so kilometres from the Kwaremont, before the long downhill stretch and that first right-hander. We all looked around and waited. By the time anyone responded, they had 15 seconds. That was enough. You're never safe, not here, not in these races.

All that, and you're not even really at the climb yet. And then you see the cobbles in front of you, and it looks laughably narrow. It's a farm track. It's a ditch cut up a field, great mud banks on either side, only just wide enough to get a team car up. There are steeper bergs. There are a few longer ones. But there aren't any that are both steep and long, and that's why it does what it does to races and racers.

They love their punchy beers round Flanders. There are several named after bergs, including one for Oude Kwaremont. And so the Kwaremont is like the blond lager that it lends its name to: not totally destructive, a powerful lager well above the usual ABV, yet one you could handle on its own. But that's the point. You never have to handle it on its own. You've ridden 200 kilometres. You've drunk one of these already, and you've drunk another ten or twelve en route. In isolation, you'd be fine – enjoying a glass with your partner over dinner, wondering what all the fuss is about. But you're not. You're on an all-dayer with the boys, and you're already teetering on the edge, and this is the one that pushes you into oblivion. Before, you were going to wake up with a bad headache. Because of the Kwaremont, you're now going to wake up in an alley or a police cell. And you'll have absolutely no idea what's going on.

You've survived the run-in. You're in the first five riders. Great. Now you have to split the climb into three sections. The first – this will be the hardest. It's 11% and the roughest part. The steepness and the cobbles want to stop you dead. You can smell the barbecues feeding the fans, smell the beer and hot dogs on their breath. There's a kerb until it disappears, and another lip comes out of nowhere.

You have to know exactly where to ride. You don't want to go down the middle. There are more cobbles missing, and they're big enough to leave the equivalent of a road divot behind. Hit one of those with your front wheel and you lose all momentum, and momentum is everything on a cobbled climb. You have to know the quickest line and accept your place along it. There's no point in swinging out wide to overtake the rider in front. Only do this if you have to; if they aren't losing the wheel, stay where you are. They're where they are for a reason. You'll hit something, slow up and go backwards. It's why the lead group will have squeezed off into a thin line of nine riders, all on each other's wheel. You might have two abreast for a few short seconds, but not for long. The further forward you are, the more chance you have of choosing your line; if you're following, follow.

One Flanders I was in second wheel, directly behind Fabian Cancellara. Perfect. I was feeling strong and able to follow his acceleration. Come on, G, this is a good day. And it was, until he caught a rider that had been out in front and went straight around him, timing his overtaking move to perfection, F1 style. Me? I didn't whip past, and I didn't time it well. I didn't get past quick enough. Off the racing line too long, my momentum lost, and suddenly, Cancellara had a 2-metre gap. And once a rider like him has that, it's so hard to close – it's like being five metres back on a flat section. Gone.

Cancellara rode away. I was left scrapping for the minor placings. And right there is the great lesson of the Kwaremont: you need to be strong, and you need good legs on the day, but your positioning is just as important. If you swing out to pass someone and can't get round them within two seconds, you're on the inferior line for longer than you want to be, you have to make a bigger effort, you're tiring and dropping back.

There's no eating, not here. You can't take your hands off the bars, and even if someone fed you like a mother bird you wouldn't be able to hold it down. You're working too hard. You'll need to have taken your last gel a good twenty minutes back, coming over the cobbled climb that precedes this, before the draggy climb on the main road and the descent into the run-in. Bang a load in there, let it kick in here, blast through the final kilometres home.

On to the second section. It levels off here, which is welcome, but also means you can relax too much. In that front group you feel safe, as if the bulk of the job is done. And that's when the guy at the front can ride away, break the chain holding him to his pursuers. He goes, you don't notice for five seconds. You look up, see him disappearing, and look at someone else to respond first so you can jump on their wheel. They're looking at someone else. The someone else is looking at you. Now there's just mud and splatter in front of you. Now you're all in trouble.

There are options here. You can ride on the verge, trust the grass, hope that the mud packed into the cracks has hardened. Some will always risk it. But you're rolling the dice, never certain where the bumps will be, a sudden patch of loose gravel, a hidden hole that sends you flying. You can think you're going to move up, only to lose twenty spots on one slip and wobble. Better to stay in the road, play the odds, stay in the game.

The final third. The road drags up again, and the fatigue from all your efforts kicks in hard. You've spent almost two minutes riding at your limit, and the climb has come back to polish you off. It's opening up on either side, the walls of fans packed behind metal barriers, and when it kicks again, you'll flick left on to a bigger road and it'll all be over. You can use the side of the road here, in the dirt, in the gravel, and if you have the legs and you're pulling away you can really increase your advantage; if your legs are going, it's the worst part of all, either a head-wind or the sensation of a headwind because everything is suddenly feeling so hard.

For now, you want to hug those barriers, even though it means more beery breath blasting you in the face when the spectators roar you on as you pass. On your last recon ride two days before you'll have seen the big beer marquees going up, and this is them delivering in style – stoking the atmosphere, taking thousands of cycling-obsessed fans to a new pitch. You can get in the gutter now, find a smoother line there than on the cobbles, hope that you don't bump an elbow or shoulder with a spectator leaning over the barriers or catch your handlebars in a coat pocket and go down like Peter Sagan did in Flanders in 2017.

It's a different noise you hear if you're at the very front or in the pack. At the front it's just wild. A beautiful kind of chaos, and that reflects itself in the racing: flat out, frantic, thrilling to be part of.

And you have to ride the cobbles right. When you're doing it well, you skim over them like a flat stone across a pond. You time it, and you almost float. When your timing is off, it's as if you've skimmed the stone at the wrong angle. It digs into the water. It drags. It dies, early. And sinks.

It suits me. I love cobbles and I like the length of this climb. It's not only for the pure power boys. Riders like Sagan, Tom Boonen and Greg Van Avermaet can punch over shorter climbs that take a minute or so; 2.2km brings riders like me into play. It's no longer just a big hit and over. You need to be able to sustain it, conserve it, go again.

The length also makes it so likely to be the start of the final race-winning move. When I won E3 in 2015, I attacked towards the bottom, rode hard from the steep part to the top with my head down. I looked around at the summit to see who was with me, and there were only two who had followed: Zdeněk Štybar and Sagan. We stayed away, I attacked again with 4km to go and got free.

The Oude Kwaremont was my launch pad. Of course, it was opportunistic; but at the same time it had been done many times before. The opportunity only becomes real if you are feeling good and you've worked that good position, going all the way back to the run-in. If you've managed all that, then this is the spot to go. Give it everything you have. See what happens. Hope, pray and pedal. And be lucky: when I won that year, I also won my own weight in that Kwaremont beer, which went down very well at my wedding in Wales that autumn.

It's not pretty, in the conventional sense. In the early-season races the landscape is bleak and harsh, as if all the colour has been stripped away. There are few trees and plenty of old farm buildings that have barely changed since the Second World War. Each little town and village has history in every cobble and crumbling brick. By the time you race the Tour of Flanders, the winter chill and darkness have been replaced by springtime warmth and birdsong. But you're still open to the elements, to the blustery wind and the rain that can sweep in across the muddy fields.

You come to ride this climb as someone who has perched on an Alpine hairpin as the Tour races by and the

Kwaremont might seem underwhelming. Like the Poggio, it's not spectacular in the way of the big snow-capped stuff. There are fewer signs. You might not even be sure you have the right road. So the way to do it is to watch classic Flanders races the week before, understand the speed of the riders, the buzz from the crowds. When you ride it, take in some of the other cobbled climbs on the way in. Let them sap your legs. And then attack the Kwaremont hard, lay down the power early on, get that all-important momentum. You can recover when it levels off, but when it opens up and begins to drag again, give it everything once more. There will be no barriers in place for you, so you can use the mud down the side when it's smooth if you like. But if you want to experience it as we do, try to stay on the cobbles all the way up. That'll give you the real feel. That'll make you feel you've truly come to terms with the Kwaremont.

I still want to go back to these races. I've turned myself into a GC rider, but I've loved Flanders since I was a kid. I've lost some of the weight I had as a Classics rider, and you sacrifice some power with that too. And you get to Tour weight by doing Tour training, and the prep for Flanders is totally different. It's not about riding uphill for ninety minutes a day. It's blasting up for thirty seconds or holding it for five. You're only rarely out of the saddle. It's seated power, and that suits me, with my old team pursuit training.

Being a little lighter does help, as it did for me in 2015. I could feel myself skipping across those cobbles in a way I hadn't before. At Paris-Roubaix weight matters less. The cobbles are big but it's all flat. So in Flanders, 70–71kg would be perfect for me: light, but with a punch. Brute force, but with knowledge of how to use it. It's brains and brawn together that conquer the Kwaremont.

Koppenberg

3/4/2015, racing Tour of Flanders
Duration: 2 mins 15 secs
Distance: 0.61km
Ave speed: 14.7kph
Ave cadence: 69
Ave heart rate: 163bpm

Size doesn't always matter, not when it comes to climbs.

The Koppenberg is only 78 metres high. That's two hairpins on Alpe d'Huez. That's one bend on the Mortirolo. It seldom comes at the right point in a race to prove decisive to the final result. It's only 600 metres long. You could fit thirty of it into the Galibier.

But there's another 'only' that matters much more with Koppenberg. It's the only climb you're likely to see elite pros getting off and walking. Sticking their bikes on their shoulders and running like it's the cyclo-cross race they have on the fields nearby in the depths of winter, or pushing them while looking like they want to punch someone.

It's got nothing to do with ability. The Koppenberg doesn't care about your prize-winners. Someone ahead of you will hit a cobble hard or at the wrong angle. The next person up brakes; you have to slow down. Then everyone's slowing down. And since you're on a slope at 25%, all your momentum evaporates in one mouthful of swear words. Someone unclips. You keep your balance and stay up but the bloke in front goes sideways into a spectator. It's wet and slimy under your wheels, so you can't get going again. And suddenly, just like that, you have a human blockage and fifty of the world's top riders all trying to walk in the sort of shoes that aren't designed for comfortable movement on carpet, let alone near-vertical lumps of polished stone.

And so this tiny little climb, over in 600m and topping out at 78m, is as iconic in cycling culture as any of the big boys in the grand tours. It's an unleasher of havoc. It's the closest you get to mountain-biking in a road race. It's like nothing else. The numbers alone don't do it justice. It's like watching snooker or darts on the TV. You see the experts, and although you accept that you'll never make a 147 or pull off a nine-dart finish, you're still sort of thinking, how hard can this really be? And then you have a pop on a full-size snooker table, and your highest break is four. You have a match and the winner is the one who concedes the fewest fouls. Twice, you actually miss the ball you're aiming at; potting any ball is so hard that each frame takes two hours, as if you're Eddie Charlton vs Cliff Thorburn.

And it's in your head, for ever. When you've ridden these Flemish roads you know all the climbs, know what comes after each one, know what the run-in is like to the next one. The races move a few around but the rhythm and the magic stay the same. All those images and memories come tumbling straight back in, even when you haven't raced them for five years.

The run-in is typical Flanders. Off the main road, more and more people moving up, 1 kilometre to a 90-degree right where you really want to be in the top five, and so find yourself in the middle of a mini bunch sprint, just as the road goes from two-and-a-half cars wide to one. Two minutes of desperate racing, almost certainly a few crashes and then a sharp 90-degree right hander to the bottom of the climb, past the white building on your left with the brown thatched roof, lobbing away heaps of momentum just when you need it more than ever.

You hear the cobbles under your wheels before you see them. Bumping, battering, ricocheting. A hundred metres of feeling the vibrations up your arms, in your elbows, in your neck and your back, and then suddenly, it lurches up at you – from 5% to 11% to 14% in 50m; then 16% and then 22%, and you're crashing into the red. Under the trees it can be wet. Early in the year there might be dead leaves to make it more slippery still, mud if it's been raced earlier that morning, dead leaves and dirt slapped down by the wheels of the team cars that have already revved their way through.

There's adrenaline racing through you – I'm on the Koppenberg! – but it's also a grind, your cadence low, your power high. On some climbs you can freewheel for a few seconds to give yourself a fraction of respite. Not here. This is like the Mortirolo; if you stop for even half a pedal stroke you will come to a halt. The steepness, the cobbles – they don't give you a second chance. It's like riding high up the banking in a velodrome and dropping below 20kph. You'll be on your backside before you know it. On the Koppenberg, if you don't keep pressure on the pedals all the time, you're done.

I've suffered the humiliation of walking up it. It was a recon ride with Team Sky, riding behind Edvald Boasson Hagen, when he started stalling and went left across the road at 45 degrees. I had to brake to avoid going into him; he straightened and kept going, I lost my momentum and had to unclip. There's always a photographer at the top of the Koppenberg, even on recon days, and sure enough he got his image. Not my proudest moment, but easily done.

Yet there's no better climb when you're feeling good, riding at the front. The atmosphere is immense. Lead the Tour of Flanders up the Koppenberg and it gives you 10 watts of power for free. It can work against the unwary – you don't want to go all in, so far from home, or you'll spend too many pennies too soon – but for the initiated, it's one of the great thrills of our sport.

It's immense, a natural amphitheatre. Steep embankments either side of the road. Spectators clinging on to the sides, drinking, cheering and desperately trying not to fall off again. Trees on top of the embankments stretching their branches out over the road, keeping the noise and madness locked in as you ride into a tunnel of craziness.

I've always looked forward to it. Seldom the fight into it, but the challenge when I'm on it – a quiet confidence that I can be as quick up there as anyone else. The history matters to me. I watched Johan Museeuw smashing up over it, Andrea Tafi powering away, and when suddenly you're on the same road, it's like travelling back in time. It could be the 1970s or the 1980s, were it not for the carbon frame between your legs. The actual conditions have barely changed; a pothole replaced here and there, some cosmetic touching up but little more. The roads in the Tour are resurfaced before we arrive. It reflects the civic pride in the race's arrival. They're smooth, laid out like a welcome carpet. This thing has barely changed in a hundred-odd years.

If this berg were a beer, it would be a punisher: 14% ABV. If you're on good form, you can handle it; of course, you'll feel it, but you can make it through. If your drinking form is instead poor, it's like meeting Mike Tyson in a bad mood: one hit and it's game over. Rather than cracking on, you'll be crawling to the nearest bench.

Despite all that it suits me. I've kept some of the high power I needed on the track, especially the seated power that the team pursuit builds in you. And I was used to doing lead-outs for the team's sprinters ever since turning pro, all the way back to the Barloworld days and our South African fast man Robbie Hunter. Holding your top end for thirty seconds, putting down two or three minutes of power – that's me.

I love the challenge these climbs bring. And the Koppenberg has been special to me – both in the rider I've been and the rider I've tried to become. If the Tour of 2015 was all about getting the high mountains right, realizing I could be a GC contender, Flanders in 2011 was when I recognized I belonged in the big one-day races. I was riding for Juan Antonio Flecha, wearing the British national champions' jersey after my win the previous summer, and I loved it – all those little efforts on the front, leading out into the climbs, still making it over the top of them in good positions, sandwiched between Filippo Pozzato and Tom Boonen, Fabian Cancellara just ahead.

And the Koppenberg was the summit to it all, chasing up the cobbles still feeling good, thinking: shit, I'm in the top fifteen here! Glued to the wheel of George Hincapie, who was always trying to win a Classic when I watched him on TV as a kid, making it over the super steep bit, buzzing off it all. The little climb that matters, and I can handle it. Just.

Netherlands

Cauberg

If Alpe d'Huez is like a massive chaotic wedding party for Dutch cycling fans, the Cauberg is the stag do. It's where they drink too much, eat only foods that have been fried and spend a whole day shouting at each other. It's where they bond, where the stories are formed that will be recounted on the big day itself, where boys become men and men act like boys all over again.

The Amstel Gold one-day classic has always been a boozy affair. There's the sponsor, and there's the fact that the first race route back in 1966 tried to take in every brewery office the company had in the Netherlands. If you don't really like cycling, it's a great excuse for an all-dayer on the sauce. If you love cycling, you do all that but on the Cauberg.

It was the first professional race I ever went to see. I'd tried to watch the Pru Tour when a stage was due to conclude in Cardiff, but an accident involving a motorbike outrider meant the finish was cancelled. They still sent Chris Boardman on ahead in his Gan jersey to say hello to the crowds, and I was still overwhelmed to see him in the flesh, running alongside him as he left the stage and headed back to his team car – 'Look! It's actual Chris

Boardman!' – but Amstel Gold had riders, atmosphere and sensational racing. I saw local favourite Michael Boogerd – the man they called Mr Cauberg – triumph in a two-up sprint against Lance Armstrong. The following year I saw the great East German Erik Zabel powering away to win in a trademark sprint of his own.

So the Cauberg has to be in this book, even if I've never personally raced up it that well. And the Cauberg, if it were to take human form, would be your classic Dutch male: lanky, likeable, sociable and slightly arrogant. 'What do you mean, the Cauberg is not in your climbing book? This is pure cycling history. So your book is a failure. Okay?'

You wouldn't say it within earshot, but without Amstel racing up it, the Cauberg might not be that significant. It's not super long; it's only 1500 metres. It's not super steep; it hits you with a ramp of 12%, but the average is closer to 5%. There's nothing crazy going on with the surface; it's good, smooth tarmac, a reddish-brown bike lane on the right-hand side, sensible Dutch road markings, sensible Dutch traffic-calming measures like chicanes and speed bumps on the way in. It's there on its own, in the otherwise unremarkable town of Valkenburg. You could ride up it on an ordinary summer's morning and wonder what all the fuss is about.

But the Cauberg knows. It's all about the history. Amstel used to finish up there, after 2003, and although (since 2017) there's now a final 19km circuit afterwards, you're still up it three times in the race. It's featured as the big climb at a World Championships on five occasions, including the 1948 version when they went up it a suicidal twenty-six times. It's Eddy Merckx winning up it, it's Philippe Gilbert winning Amstel again and again, it's Mathieu van der Poel charging up it en route to winning Amstel twenty-nine years after his dad, Adri.

I first rode the Cauberg as a junior, in a race held the same day as the big boys' one. I thought I knew it from my trips as a fan, but I didn't, not really. The noise from the fans was astonishing. You could hear the race commentary crackling out of the PA speakers hanging off lampposts every 200m. You could hear music and smell the hot dogs and the sponsor's foaming product.

The run-in is quick. You come down a fast road into town, swing a long, steady left and then begin to climb. It's a shallow start, an S-bend left and then an S-bend right, and you swing past bars, restaurants and houses with people hanging out of the windows.

It's a mad rush into the climb for positioning, a slight lull as the road bends and then the anticipation of attacks to come. Sometimes guys attack off the front or just to the side, at the point you're looking over your shoulder expecting the danger to come from the rear. If you don't have the legs to follow, the road will find you out, because it's 9% for a stretch of around 100m and then maybe double that at 11%. Just like the Cipressa and Poggio, on its own it's nothing special. But after a gruelling day of Dutch bergs, it'll quickly find you out.

It can seem more controlled than similar climbs in Belgium, smoother, cleaner. Belgium is raw and rough and ready – literally with its cobbles and metaphorically in its character. On the Cauberg the fans are behind metal barriers. It does seem to be national Bring A Flag To Work Day, but there's a separation between rider and spectator. In Belgium you're all as one. The fans are part of the actual race, not just half-cut window dressing. The road here is wider, and it works for the GC men – more of a normal race compared to the Kwaremont or Koppenberg, a place where you can still move up on the outside rather than needing to choose exactly the right line or go backwards.

But you still need a punchy kick in your legs. For a short climb it drags, under the bridge that goes overhead, another 300m from the summit to the finish line in those early 21st century days. There is a truth to climbs like this: if you don't have enough, you can't fake it, and if you do have what it takes, there's little anyone else can do about it. It's why Gilbert had so much success; like Richie Porte on Willunga, we all knew where he was going to attack and how; we just weren't able to do anything about it.

It's a great example to follow, if you can. I rode the team time-trial there in the Worlds of 2012 and had a shocker, dropping my chain around halfway through the race. I couldn't get back to the group, and had to ride to the finish out the back on my own, watching other teams fly past me. And so the Cauberg felt like the Alpe then, me slogging away, the fans still roaring but me unable to respond, my race over.

A couple of years later I rode Amstel but was taken out when a rider ahead decided to swerve across the road to take a leak by the side. Nor was it a slow, controlled curve to the pavement. It was as if he were taking a 90-degree corner coming up to a finish line; I didn't see him until his back wheel was where my front one should have been.

Down I went. Taking the piss on a hill where everyone else gets on it.

Mallorca

Sa Calobra

The thing about most climbs in this book is that you climb them. They're about going up, as an elite rider, not going back down. I've never descended the way we go up Alpe d'Huez. I've never gone down the Mortirolo, or the Stevio or Solden, not on a bike.

And so Sa Calobra is different, not only because of those tight turns and the one they call the Tie-Knot, the one that goes back over itself like the slip road at a complicated motorway junction. It's different in that it's a dead end, so it's always a descent first, unless you want to stick your bike on one of the little boats that shuttles tourists round from Port de Sóller – and sticking your bike on a boat is not something that Dave Brailsford really approves of.

It's a descent, and it's a destination. You don't accidentally find Sa Calobra. It's not part of a loop. You turn off the C710 road through the Tramuntana mountains, dive down and get ready to come straight back up again. Because of that it can be hard on the head. You can't enjoy the descent when you know how quickly you'll have to repay that debt, and you'll find it even more challenging if you're a track specialist who usually goes round and round rather than up and down. Word on the Mallorcan street was that Steven Burke and Wendy Houvenaghel, while not as cautious on descents as triathletes, clocked very similar times for their ascent and descent.

It can also get pretty cold. When you're sizzling in Sóller or toasty in Pollença you think a short-sleeved jersey might be a bit much. You swoop down Sa Calobra having ridden through rain at the top and you can spend the next 10km shivering uncontrollably. Stick a gilet in the back pocket. Consider arm-warmers. Trust me.

But I don't want to put you off. Sa Calobra is a beauty. Mallorca was the first place outside Wales I ever rode my bike, as a junior accustomed to the punchy but brief climbs accessible on a day trip from Cardiff, and it blew my mind. It was a whole new world – climbs that took forty minutes to get up, climbs where the sun shone and the sea sparkled blue in the distance and the road kept going, and you could kid yourself that you had been dropped into the sharp end of a Tour de France stage. I used to throw myself down Sa Calobra. I'd push it into every corner. I'd get caught out sometimes by the ones towards the bottom that tighten up on you with no warning, be forced to swing wide and thank my lucky stars that no cars happened to be coming the other way at the same time. If I ever came close to forgetting the dangers, I'd have a quick glance to my right just after the natural rock tunnel towards the bottom and see a smashed-up bus on the rocks down below. It must have been there for a good two years before it was moved, and while I'm not a hundred per cent sure how or why it ended up there, it couldn't have been good.

Yet I loved the start of the climb back up, deep blue sea behind, the squeeze through the rock formations that lean in so close and high on either side that you think they might squash the life out of you. I'd be out of the saddle, flicking the bike around past the trees leaning over the road and the massive boulders that appeared to have stopped for no reason and could keep rolling at any moment, and I'd think, whoah, this is a whole new world.

Seven hundred metres of altitude gain, a maximum gradient of almost 13%. I know it as well as any other climb in the world because I must have ridden it fifty times now. I've been on training camps to Mallorca with the Great Britain track team and with Sky and Ineos at least once a year since 2004, at least twice a year in half of those. Every time we ride in Mallorca, we ride Sa Calobra. It's the dead end you return to again and again.

The track-specific sessions were a horror: twenty seconds hard, forty seconds recovery. That was a good day. The bad day was twenty hard, twenty off. Because the recovery and the off are still on a slope of more than 7%. They're a tough effort in their own right. You'd begin your first set at the bottom, finish it wasted and then see a sign telling you there were eight kilometres of climbing still to come.

Like any rider, I would search for what little consolation could be found. In the velodrome in Palma, Ed Clancy could make the rest of us in the team pursuit quartet look like lightweights. When we practised standing starts he would smash out his half-lap a second faster than we could manage, and then roll round the bottom of the track laughing at me attempting a massively over-geared start. Happily, the same attributes that worked for him on the boards worked against him on steep tarmac, so Brad Wiggins and I would take pleasure in looking back down the road from two hairpins up and throwing gels at his pale, sweaty face. Our coach, Matt Parker, would take pity on him and try to help, although I'm not sure how much motor-pacing uphill at 5kph actually does.

These days, training for 6-hour races rather than 3 minutes 51 seconds, our efforts are longer, less intense and every bit as hard. They'll set them up as a handicap, knowing what our instinctive competitiveness will drag out of us. It doesn't matter whether you're chasing down the guy in front or trying to hold off the flying South Americans behind. Either way, you push too hard and the last couple of kilometres are sickening. Focus on the view; let the legs take care of themselves.

The bottom is the steepest part. It then settles down, allowing the non-track specialist to get into their groove, before it jumps up again towards the end. The road itself is not, however, your only menace. There's the wind, which can slap you about with proper gusts towards the top. There are the tour buses, which thunder down and then crawl back up on summer afternoons. When the GB team were training in Mallorca ahead of the London Olympics in 2012, we were forced out of bed at an hour that track riders seldom see, all to avoid the thousands of tourists who pile down there on summer afternoons. You work for a lifetime to make an Olympics; you train relentlessly for the four years that precede them. Losing all that to a coachload of German OAPs is not part of the Lottery-funded plan.

It's also a decent ride in, whether you're coming from Sóller, Pollença or Inca. There are climbing miles in your legs before you've even officially begun. You're never completely fresh on Sa Calobra. I remember doing it with Brad one December on a big loop from Pollença around the flatter roads, then up Sóller, the Puig and finally Sa Calobra. Except 'finally' turned out to be off the mark.

Both of our training programmes were track-oriented then, so this was an especially big ride. So as we approached the descent of Sa Calobra, the debate was aired.

'Oooh, do we really need to do this?'

'Yeah, come on, these are the days that count . . .'

So down we went, a U-turn and straight back up, cresting to the top, dehydrated and hungry, but in joyful mood.

'Great day that, mate.'

'Big-time. Proper box ticked.'

'Just a long descent home to Port Pollença now.'

'Lovely.'

That was the moment when we swung round a corner to be confronted by a massive landslide, boulders the size of minibuses piled up across the road. No way was it passable. Trust me, we tried. Which meant we had to ride back up the Puig and all the way down to Sóller, try to get home that way. It was late, the sun setting early anyway. Despite it being 2007, neither of us had bothered bringing a phone, or indeed any money. So when we limped back to Sóller and found one of the few restaurants still open, we had to borrow their phone and call Brad's wife, Cath, back in Lancashire, on the basis that it was the only number we could remember. Cath had to ring the velodrome in Manchester to get a coach's number. She then had to ring the coach, Dan Hunt, to tell him where we were. By the time Dan turned up in his car, tired from the long drive, angry at the call-out, we'd piled through two coffees, four Cokes, two mains and a dessert – the cyclist equivalent of the Very Hungry Caterpillar. 'Hey Dan! We've got no money, could you pay the bill as well?'

So those pros who have the best times up it tend to be the ones arriving with form, rather than the Europeans arriving in December after an enjoyable off-season in which they ate all the things cyclists aren't supposed to eat and washed them down with drinks they're not supposed to drink. Richie Porte has flown up it, after training for the Aussie national champs, and with an accommodating sea breeze at his back. Brad set a decent time up it before the Tour in 2012. The South Americans are always impressive; those boys never truly lose their climbing form.

I'll go back there when I'm retired, ride down once again and then stop for coffee and a long lunch. Maybe I'll meet Chris Hoy, who named one of his range of road bikes after the climb, despite going up it as often as I've had caviar for tea. If a team pursuiter like Ed Clancy can seem slow going up Sa Calobra, imagine what a man who specialized in going flat out for 250 metres made of it. Although even Chris was faster uphill than his fellow Olympic gold medalist Phil Hindes. It's a marathon not a sprint, this one.

Puig Major

The world moves on fast. One moment everyone's talking about Ma-jorka, the next it's all My-yorker. And yet we still refer in cycling circles to a climb called the Pig, and it's really not a pig, linguistically or metaphorically.

A pig is a filthy animal. The Puig is far from filthy. It's pleasant to look at. There are trees and blue skies and usually a very amenable temperature. It's fourteen kilometres long, but at an average of just over 6%, and that's aggressive but not dirty. Sa Calobra is nastier. Sa Calobra has the grunt and the teeth.

And yet. The Puig is not domesticated. It's a bear – not a grizzly that's going to eat you, but a tame-ish one that you can approach safely if you're cautious. And that's the key element: vigilance. Be respectful. A bear can be cuddly, but it's still a bear. In the same way as Wales hooker Scott Baldwin now regrets putting his hand through the bars of a lion's cage at Weltevreden Game Lodge in South Africa, you don't try to pet the Puig. Forget a nip on the hand, as Scott experienced. The Puig will bite you on the arse.

You can ride it from west or east, from Sóller or Pollença. It's fun both ways but it's the Sóller version that is the classic – a lovely Vilaflor vibe, nice bit of tree cover to shelter from the direct sunlight, fun, twisty road, views from all angles. It's the one that gets the heart beating when you realize, as a kid from Cardiff, that it's genuinely possible to ride uphill for forty minutes without being on a turbo trainer with your front wheel on a pile of books. That 6% gradient is almost perfect if you're tootling up it, enough of a slope to push against but with no need to feel truly uncomfortable. You can sit on someone's wheel and admire the scenery and suck the fresh air into your lungs. You can pull alongside them and chat in sentences of more than three words. It's a holiday on a bike. A working holiday, but still.

From the Pollença side, it's a completely different vibe. Fewer trees, more tunnels. Reservoirs, more wind, the looming presence of the military base in the distance. It's more grim this side, especially in December. You could be high up in the Alps here, well above 2000m.

Either way, the road feels quick under your wheels. It's a different tarmac to the UK, the stuff they lay down in the Balearics. It's less grippy, more polished. It's smooth and fast and shiny when the sun's out and an absolute horror of a skidpan when it's wet. Mallorcan roads in the rain may be the most treacherous in the world. I remember a knockabout training race when I was there with the GB under-twenty-three academy, and both the Welsh squad for the 2006 Commonwealth Games and the GB Olympic track team were staying in the same hotel. A race that began in the sunshine and ended in a demolition derby in the rain. Every corner of every descent either had a British rider twitching their back wheel round it or sliding across it on their burning backside.

There are cars on the Puig, but not many, and because they expect riders, and may well be riders themselves, they tend to give you space and consideration. There are riders everywhere, some of them professional, others decent amateurs. It is good to see them all, but certain protocols must be maintained. If you're a pro on a long general ride, not eating much, cruising, you struggle to look kindly on the ones who sprint on to your back wheel and then take videos of your sweaty arse. It's like someone coming into the office where you're working over a particularly tedious spreadsheet and just staring over your shoulder. Better to say a quick hello, enjoy a minute of stimulating chat and then drop back. What you should never do is try to prove your credentials by racing us. We're not racing. We have probably done more miles today, and yesterday, and tomorrow. We see you as fellow travellers, not bitter Grand Tour rivals.

Worse still is when I wave to say hello to a rider going past in the other direction, as is customary in the UK, only to find them slamming on the brakes and chasing back up to us. The wave signifies politeness. It says, 'How are you doing?' What it doesn't say is, 'Hey mate, come and ride with us for an hour, nearly crashing into us every corner.' One chap even tried riding in the middle of our group on the descent of the Puig. Politely, we tried asking him to head his own way, at least until we came around a corner to a set of roadworks and a big red light, when he almost ended up hitting a car. Luckily, that sort of chat is rare. We're all cyclists. We're all friends. You enjoy your riding vibe, we'll enjoy ours.

It's the same with e-bikes. Absolutely nothing wrong with them – a great way of getting more people out riding, of getting more people to 1500m summits like the Puig. But do not use those free watts to coast alongside a rider burying themselves in pursuit of some distant future title. Big efforts, 500-watt efforts, can take you to dark places. Suffering in silence is one thing. Suffering while a man twice your weight half-wheels you with only the occasional proper push on the pedals is just sadism.

There's a certain look for riders on the Puig. German, late forties, solid tan, pink and white T-Mobile jersey from 2008. That's magic. You see groups of five or ten mates, all in the same retro jerseys from Prendas; you see lone stragglers, wearing the same tattered jersey they've been sporting on every single ride for the past twenty years; you see club riders in their flashy latest design, on a jolly in the sunshine but a training jolly. I've yet to work out the one stigma in cycling that continues to hang around: the notion that it's somehow wrong to wear the jersey of your favourite team. You do it for football, rugby, NFL, even cricket. Rock the kit you love. That's what I say.

You roll off the Puig into one of the villages on its southern flanks – Caimari, Selva, Moscari – and the streets appear deserted until you turn a corner into the square and suddenly, there are cyclists everywhere, all drinking great orange juice and average coffee and piling into panini. Truly, you can be a cyclist without shame on the Puig. Just don't order an ice cream, as Ian Stannard did when we rode with T-Mobile as juniors. It's only really a holiday for those on the beach.

Portugal

Malhão

21/02/2016, winning Volta ao Algarve
Duration: 7 mins 11 secs
Distance: 2.39km
Ave speed: 19.8kph
Ave heart rate: 171bpm
Ave power: 455w
Note: my best ever power output over seven minutes is
482w, during stage fourteen of the Tour in 2018, the final
climb in the Mende stage, when I would have weighed
around 68.5/69kg. In the Algarve, earlier in the year, I
weighed around 71kg. You can see the big difference in
the power to weight ratio.

Sometimes a climb could be anywhere in the world. It's just a steep road that makes your legs hurt. Others could only be in one place; they're everything about that country in one lung-busting effort.

That's Malhão. We ride it in the Volta ao Algarve each February, and it's southern Portugal in every aspect. Green hills, at that time of year, low white houses, blue skies. There's the fact that it's a burst of warm winter sun, that it's important but still relaxed, that there are almost as many overseas accents as the strange local one that sounds like Russian but isn't. It's not flashy – it's Cédric Soares rather than Cristiano Ronaldo – but it's easy on the eye, and you're glad to be there and happy to be back.

And it's a solid little climb. Two and a half kilometres long, climbing up to 500 metres, topping out at almost 9% gradient. When it hurts you, there's the temptation to remind it that it's February not June, and if you were to come back when you're not carrying a few extra kilos and your power was where it should be, then it would be a different matter; but you never feel like an argument with Malhão, because it's not that sort of vibe. You've had a couple of sprinters' days in the race, a time-trial, and now this is the big day to wrap it all up. Nice to see you again, how's your winter been?

It's a great way to start the year. A little of everything, race-wise; nothing too hard, serious or dangerous; the same hotel for the entire week, the sun on our backs. We even get to experience Malhão twice, just as you do Willunga in Tour Down Under: the first time to soften the legs, a hard lap around shorter, steeper climbs in the area and then a flat-out battle up to the top once more.

It's a quick run-in to the bottom, slightly downhill, and then a sharp right-hander and you're on it. It's quick because of that downhill but also because your position in the bunch matters when it kicks up to 10%. The hulking mass of the mountain is on your right so the wind can come stiff from the left, and here it's about riding hard but holding something back as the less experienced go all in. The pace will spike; it's the set-piece climb. You will ride a little quicker than you want. But don't be dragged into the red – try to spin the legs; avoid sticking it in too big a gear and getting bogged down in a grindfest; concentrate on keeping your breathing smooth and relaxing your upper body.

Now you're working your way round to the left, and it opens up even more. The gradient starts to shallow off, and those who went too hard too soon start going backwards. You swing round a long, slow 90-degree turn and it kicks up again for 200 metres. Attacks will come now. Look over your shoulder, look for the twitch in a rival's muscles, the way they edge slightly forward in the saddle or shift their hands on the bars. One more tight left-hander and you can see the top. Be glad of the breeze. Be glad you're racing at the front, because if it hurts for you, it hurts even more for those in your wake.

There's no blagging it on Malhão. You've either done the work and laid off the desserts during the off-season and you're there, in front, fighting for something . . . or you're not. Some climbs you can kid yourself – 'Ah, I'm okay, actually.' Not Malhão. Malhão will expose you.

But enjoy it, if you can. The Volta is to Portugal what the Tour of Britain is to the UK. It's the biggie. And anyone who cares about cycling will have made the effort to come along and watch. You might not think about Portugal when you think about European cycling, but you should; it's produced a world champion in Rui Costa, and stage winners at each of three Grand Tours. There will always be a Portuguese rider in the top five of the GC here, and there will be smaller local teams who are thrilled to be racing alongside big-name World Tour outfits, just as I used to be when I first got selected for proper stage races.

There will be teams you haven't heard of before and teams that you think are called something else, because you see the name of a sponsor on one sleeve and assume that's their name, rather than a company who produce hot tubs in the wider Vilamoura area and want to get this fact on nationwide television. You might spot a memorable logo on the other sleeve and spend the whole race talking into your team radio about an attack from the Sharks or the Cheese Slices. You might get obsessed with the whole jersey and spend an hour of easy pedalling trying to work out which three World Tour teams they have borrowed significant design ideas from.

A strange contradiction: I've won the Volta ao Algarve twice, but I've never had an amazing day up Malhão. I've done enough but no more, never flown up it. The first time I raced it, Alberto Contador disappeared into the distance, but it was what Steve Cummings was doing behind him, and then next to him, and then ahead of him, that stuck with me. Steve was the great example. He was the GB track rider who switched to the road and made it work, even before Brad Wiggins, even outside time-trials. I watched his training change, watched how he worked on the roads in Mallorca. On this day he got his tactics spot on, in a way that we would all borrow from in future years. 'G, I didn't go in the red like I normally do; I let them ride away. Then around halfway they eased up and I got back to the front. I then won the sprint at the top, but it was more of an attack from 300m out.' And he's right. That's how you win up Malhão.

Years later, when I was defending my leader's jersey, Richie Porte was the man with magic legs. He'd had a bad time-trial and so was way down in GC, but his form was good after his usual deeds at Tour Down Under and Willunga. So he piloted me beautifully through the rapid chase into the bottom of the climb, took me to within 500 metres of the top with only four other riders for company, and then gave me a shout: G, all right if I go for the stage?

Yes mate. You go. Have fun. That's what Malhão's about.

Australia

Willunga

It's Old Willunga Hill, to give it its official title. But what they should actually call it – what we all call it in the team – is Richie's Hill.

Tour Down Under, every January, in and around Adelaide, almost always with Richie Porte winning up it. Always posting the best times on Strava, always attacking in the same place. He's the Muhammad Ali of Willunga. He has the reputation; he has the record.

He's got help on his side. It's January, it's Australia. So if you're Australian, and January is your summer, of course you're going to be in shape. I'm not built to cope with the South Australian climate in summer. It's too hot for too long. I find myself thinking wistfully of rain-soaked Valley roads. If we raced Willunga in March, you'd have more riders on his wheel. You might even have a few going past. He'd still win, because it's Richie's Hill, but it would be tighter. The gap at the top would be smaller.

Willunga is one of those climbs that hurts because of its context. It's not even that long, at well under four kilometres. It averages 7%, even if there are cheeky ramps within that. But it comes on the sixth day of Tour Down Under, and six days of racing right at the start of the season is quite the post-Christmas wake-up call. And so the race into the bottom of the climb is equal parts frantic, aggressive and weary – a big old scrap for the front that can spit you out the back before you know it.

It's a long, straight road into the town of Willunga, and the wind blows straight across it. Nothing detonates a nice orderly peloton like a crosswind. One moment you're rolling along in a loose flying-V shape, the next you're spread out across the road in splintered echelons, yelling and arguing with each other. When there's a headwind on that road it's almost worse. Then you have riders working flat out to get to the front, only to take the wind straight in the chops, fight it briefly and then drop back defeated. No one able to stay there, a constant chopping and changing that leads to more yelling and feistier arguments.

Even on a calm day there's a skittishness in the air. No rider wants to be stuck halfway down the field coming on to Willunga, so there is a relentless washing-machine motion in the peloton – guys out of the saddle, charging up the outside, trying to find room in the brown dirt off the side of the tarmac. You need looking after by your teammates. Too many are risking too much. Gambling on getting their front wheel into a little space that suddenly closes up in front of them, going into the red, blowing up and then drifting backwards as the next man makes his charge. Sometimes you're better riding it Simon and Adam Yates style, leaving it until the last moment to make your move to the front. It's riskier but if you can make it stick, you'll have energy for the real business of the climb that others may not.

It kicks up fast, Willunga. Straight off the high street, 9% for the first kilometre. That gradient usually brings a measure of calm. You're all sussing each other out. One team might take it on, but they'll never go full gas. Every now and then you might get a maverick move from a European rider who gets fooled by the blue skies and sunshine and suddenly thinks they're in the Alps in July, but their legs soon remind them of their error and they're back in the peloton with a chastened expression and philosophical shake of the head.

It's all about not going too deep, this first part. If you feel yourself overheating, back off. It can be hard to get enough carbs down you on the way in to Willunga; the heat takes away your appetite, and the high-carb drinks we have just make me more thirsty. You'll want to throw your bottle away at the bottom of the climb to save weight, so drink all day. Stick an extra hydro tablet in your ordinary drink, keep the electrolytes coming. It's the dry heat that gets you on Willunga, that feeling of standing in front of a hairdryer, of your face and fingers being crusty from the sweat and the residue of energy gels. It can feel claustrophobic, as if you can't escape it. And if the flies fancy you ... look, in Wales, if you swat a fly, it clears off sharpish; swat a fly in Australia and it goes off to tell all its mates to come at you, too. 'He can only take one hand off the bars on this hill – you go in for his right eye, I'll go left.'

Now the gradient drops a little, back to 7%. The road surface is smooth under your wheels but heavy, and the heat makes it feel stickier. You're exposed to the sun in the first half and by the time the trees begin to come into view you're already half-cooked. For Richie, this is the signal to go. Same spot, same attack, same result. For those without his legs, you try to let the distinctive shapes and smells of the peeling eucalyptus trees distract you a little. If you've got Bernie Eisel with you, you might have some local wildlife pointed out to you. Bernie has the ability to spot a koala on a branch from a half a mile away.

The third kilometre and the gradient eases again, down towards 6%, the fans roaring you on from the shade of the trees. The last 500 metres are easier still, as you swing round to the left and the top, but by this point you're just watching Richie's backside, if you're lucky enough to still be that close. Only the jersey he's wearing changes with the years. And then there's the plateau at the summit, and more crosswinds, and a drag along the top before you swing left once more and begin the super-fast descent back to the main road and the straight run-in to Willunga.

It's a brutal little thing. It's not long, like a big climb in the Tour, and it's not as steep as some of the Belgian bergs. But it's punchy, hard and hot, always a big, hard effort, and you need those noisy fans to keep you going. It's wine from McLaren Vale in the comfortable hospitality tents at the bottom, stubbies from Eskies at the top, three or four deep in the final kilometre and a half. It's Australia's version of Alpe d'Huez. Fancy dress everywhere, inflatable kangaroos, paint on the road. And the fans love it – the only World Tour race within about five time zones, and even then you'll only have one in China, and who wants to watch a bike race there? So they come from far and wide to let rip, and boy do you know about it. Plenty of snarky shouts about Poms, which is going to happen when the GB track cycling team has repeatedly done what it has to the Australian one, but solid support, too. There's a camaraderie between British and Aussie fans, even if neither side is ready to admit it. You like sport? Yeah, so do I. You like beer? What, you too?

In 2013, I'd left the track behind and was committing to the road. The Tour Down Under was my first target: start the year with a bang, get the momentum and see where it takes me. Fine, except when you want to perform at that time of year, there's no long general easy rides in November and December with the odd fifteen minutes at zone three. Instead there's sprints, repeated capacity efforts, twenty-minute blocks of threshold on the rolling road near Pollença in Mallorca. It's full-on, but it has to be if you want to be competitive against those flying Aussies. As the years went by, my goals changed and so did my emphasis on the results page in Adelaide, but

I still loved it. It was a great way to start the year. I'd head out a good couple of weeks before the race, leaving just after Christmas and all the extra distractions that brings, have a good training block in beautiful weather followed by a good week of racing, then head back to Europe ready to go.

Yet I've never had a truly great ride up Willunga when we've been racing. I'd look at Richie's segment times on Strava and feel intimidated. But in 2013, I was riding well and in the leader's jersey after winning the stage up Corkscrew Road, which is shorter but steeper. My old Sky teammate Simon Gerrans said he'd look out for me on Willunga, as long as it didn't ruin his own chances. So I sat on his wheel, and I was fine through the first two kilometres, right to the Richie attack point. And when Simon went there, because he's not stupid, I couldn't follow. I was already on my limit. He even gave me a shout over his shoulder. 'Come on, G!' But it was Simon Geschke who went with him instead, Gerrans who kept the Aussie stranglehold on the stage and me who finished third.

Simon's a good man. Most of the Aussies in the bunch are as you'd expect: quite aggressive, like to think of themselves as tough, friendly but also a bit chippy. That's Willunga too. It's not nasty but it has an edge. You can get along with it, but you're never totally accepted. It likes to push you, and it prefers it if you buckle. And if Richie wins.

Tenerife

Bumpy

Right. Prepare to be confused. The Bumpy climb is not called the Bumpy climb. You ask a local on Tenerife to direct you there and they won't have a clue, even if they grew up on it. It's just called the Bumpy climb within a select group of cyclists who have ridden it endless times, and we call it the Bumpy climb because the road surface is so bumpy.

Except it's not. Not any more. The municipal authorities resurfaced it some time ago. So the Bumpy climb, which isn't the Bumpy climb, isn't even bumpy these days.

But these things stick. There's a road near where I lived as a kid in Cardiff that we used to call Red Road, on account of the colour of the tarmac. It was repaved when I was sixteen and has thus been a standard black road for eighteen years. We still call it Red Road. It's like your mate at school who got the nickname Cheddar after eating an entire block of Cheddar cheese in Tesco at 3am after your first night out. He's never done it since, and, in fact, doesn't even like cheese. But you still call him Cheddar, and so does everyone else. There are people from his uni who don't even know his real name, only finding out when the vicar at his wedding starts banging on about some bloke called Ian.

This is the Bumpy climb. Neither was it the only bumpy climb on Tenerife when we first began training on the island. Almost all the roads were in a terrible shape. This was just the worst. And we had to ride it so often that it was always on our minds – uphill, to get back to our hotel towards the top of Mount Teide, downhill, if we were turning left out of the hotel to take on the climbs around Vilaflor and Chirche.

In our early days on Tenerife there was no Google Maps on our phones. There weren't even many paper maps of the island. It added a fresh dimension to the route planning of Tim Kerrison. No Wi-Fi in the hotel, phone signal in only five of the thirty-seven rooms. Where were we? Where were we going? Were there no steamrollers in the Canaries?

This was the worst way home by far. We used to hate it. Coming up it you'd be weaving around, trying to avoid all the potholes. As a descent it had the sort of gradient and heaviness under your wheels that meant you had to pedal going down, and that never sits comfortably with a rider. There was usually a headwind, and the road was so bad after the descent you'd feel like you'd just ridden a couple of secteurs of Paris-Roubaix. The only way it could get worse would be if it was raining, and because Tenerife's weather is a succession of seemingly unrelated microclimates, we had that a lot, too. There was a time when we set off in freezing sideways rain – me, Chris

Froome, Wout Poels and Vasil Kiryienka – and it was so deeply unpleasant that Kiri stopped by the side of the road. We discussed it. 'Boys, what should we do here?' In that brief interim, Kiri had made his decision, turned around and gone home. When a man from Belarus considers conditions overly bleak you know you're in trouble. Meanwhile, Tim kept insisting that in a few kilometres all would be fine. He spoke of warm sunshine and soft sea breezes. Yeah right, we thought. 'It's not that bad, guys; the temperature gauge in the car says it's 6°C!' Hmm, so if it's that in a nice warm car . . . Thing is, we then turned a corner and he was absolutely spot on. It was a delight. Except for the bumps, but still.

And so it's hard to forget the way Bumpy used to be, even now it's a changed climb. Forget Cheddar. Bumpy is the sort of character who used to be a right idiot at school, always getting in trouble, kicking everyone when you played football in the playground, never getting the ball, never bothered about getting the ball. And then when you meet him years later, he's suddenly all polite and courteous, handshakes and smiles. He's got a girlfriend who also seems lovely. Your own partner is so charmed she refuses to accept, when you talk about it in the car afterwards, that he could ever have been an arse. It almost makes you angry. Trust me, he's not like that really. You don't know.

So this is Bumpy, today and for ever: long straights,

grinding away, never punishingly steep but always dragging, a place that's good for an effort, for no other reason than it means you go quicker and so get it done sooner. We'll often do a team effort up here, the aim being to deliver the leader or whoever is particularly strong that day to a predetermined finish line. It's not pleasant. After a big day out it hurts. But they give you something to concentrate on, so the kilometres tick by so much faster.

There have been times, conversely, when I've been completely empty. No energy, no morale. And when that happens, there is no worse road in the world. It's so lonely. It's so long. I've seen Kiri slow to 10kph and still refuse to take any food from the car or even jump in for a ride. We took half an hour out of him in 10km, and still he rode on. Hard. Despite the weather story.

The kilometre markers don't help when you're feeling vulnerable. The top of the climb is at 4km, since the road flattens out and slowly descends through the lava fields, and it counts down rather than up, so you start your effort at 32km. That feels like a big number when you're tired from the day before and you can feel every mile you've ridden over the training camp sitting heavy in your legs. It's so long that at the bottom you can not only see the coast and the beaches in the distance but imagine what it would be like to be drinking lager on them. There are palm trees when you begin, pines halfway up and then a nothingness as you climb into the lava fields. And then it's just bleak – spectacular, for sure, but windy – and bad thoughts can leak into your head. The first time you ride through it, you think, whoah, this is pretty cool. The places my bike can take me! Two weeks in, when the only variety in your eyeline is whether that lump of black rock is slightly bigger than the one next to it, you're dreaming of the soft landscapes you grew up on, the leafy lanes and hedges of your youth. You try not to dwell on the fact that Teide is still an active volcano. You try not to think of the lava pouring out of the crater in red-hot form, or that Teide has historically erupted every 200 or so years, and the last time was about 200 years ago. Let's stay calm here, there are fifty-two weeks in the year, we're here for four, am I that unlucky?

And yet you come to grow fond of it, in a strange way. It is like nowhere else you ever go. The air is thin and clean and fresh. It's incredibly quiet. There are almost no people about, once the coaches taking tourists on stargazing tours have gone away again. You ride the roads and you see the volcano from different angles as the roads wind around it, and you think of six-year-old Geraint in Birchgrove reading about volcanos in books, and here you are actually on one.

All of which makes it more shameful that in the thirty-six-odd cumulative weeks I've spent there, I've never taken the little cable car to the actual top. You can see it from my hotel room window. We get days off. Each time

I go back I convince myself that this will be the time. And yet it never is. I don't even know why. I don't have all the answers.

There are plenty of other pro teams training on Bumpy. There are plenty staying in the same hotel. But that emptiness, the vastness of the landscape, is reflected in how infrequently we meet. In all the times I've climbed Bumpy, I've only ever done it once at the same time as another team, and that was Astana, and we were on a big effort, so we passed them, which was encouraging. You can be there for two weeks and never see another rider. And then on the last day you go to the little bike storage room out the back and bump into eight Italians, four Dutchmen and a pair of Russians. It's the most awkward conversation of the year, forced surprise and jollity, no one wanting to give away any training secrets. And you're all best of mates, until a week later when you're all at a race in France and swearing and chopping each other up.

Oh. For the record, if you are trying to find the Bumpy climb, it's the TF-38. And then the TF-21. But it's always Bumpy to me.

Vilaflor

The way you think about a climb is not always the way a climb deserves to be thought about. When you race up a climb, you make a snap judgment. Performed well? You like it. Had a stinker? Hate it.

When you train up a climb instead, you're a better judge of character. You have the opportunity to get to know its true nature. You're balanced and you're fair. It's not about me, it's about you.

That's why Vilaflor on Tenerife is one of my favourites. There may be three routes to the little town and the final climb to the top, but they all work for me. We've spent a lot of time together, down the years. I've had good days, I've had bad days. The climbs have stayed the same.

The three options to Vilaflor bring a natural variety. The coffee you have in the town towards the end of the long day looping up and down them puts a zip in your legs and a smile on your face. (That's purely due to the caffeine – the actual coffee is nothing to write home about; not as bad as the French but not far off, unless you're having a café bombón, which is an espresso plus a good squeeze of sugary condensed milk. If this doesn't work as a pick-me-up, you should head to the nearest hospital as something is seriously wrong with you.) The sun is usually shining, you're in a training group with your mates and you're on a volcanic island 200 miles off the coast of west Africa. You're far from the troubles of the world and long enough away from the stresses of the racing calendar not to worry about what might happen down a French descent or in a Swiss time-trial in a few months' time.

I first rode this climb in 2011. It was our first altitude camp as a team, all focused on Brad Wiggins and the goal of trying to win our first Tour de France. I'd ridden the big mountains of the Alps and Pyrenees before, but that first drive up the mountain, from the airport in the south to our hotel on the top, was rather daunting – forty-five minutes of grinding away, with one thought in a loop in our heads: 'Are we genuinely riding this most days?'

From Vilaflor to the top is thirteen kilometres, most of it twisting through the forests, clean air in your lungs, road smooth under your wheels. So much to see and smell and soak in that the kilometres flick past in a way they never do on the Bumpy climb. It's just a question of which route you choose to get you there:

1. La Camella. Without wanting to puncture the good mood, this may be the worst ride on the entire island. The road might be the last one the civic authorities have got round to resurfacing. Sixteen

kilometres at an average gradient of 6% shouldn't feel this bad, but with the tarmac as heavy as a retired prop and as lumpy as his ears, it annoys you on a good day and makes you curse on a bad one.

2. San Miguel. The central of the three options, steep and hard yet satisfying, constantly changing in gradient. Take the TF-563 through El Fronton; be grateful you're not on La Camella.

3. Grenadilla. The most pleasant option. The road surface on the TF-21 is a beauty; the road twists and turns so you're never bored; the gradient stays steady at around 5% for almost all of its 13km. There are terraced fields on your right, the sea behind you, the sun on your back.

There's an easy rhythm to days on these roads. All of us out together, the last efforts of a long day in the saddle, maybe one ascent via San Miguel, drop down to Grenadilla, back up, back down, once more out of the saddle and up. A coffee in Vilaflor, then the final stretch ridden as if we're deep in a Grand Tour and working our way up the final climb to a summit finish. Luke Rowe will take it on at the front of the pace line with instructions to bury himself for the first 4km. If he can do more, if the coffee's working, he'll go further. When his goose is cooked, the next man takes over. Each has their target, each has their role. With 2km to go it's me and Froomey, time-trialling it out to the top and finishing with a sprint for the imaginary line. All the time the shade keeping us cool, all the while the sea breezes coming up from the crowded resorts and beaches down below and taking a little more perspiration off the brow. The team effort can hurt. Not everyone enjoys having the hurt put on them. But it gets more out of each one of us, for we are born-and-bred racers, and you give us a reason and scenario that make sense and we can go all in.

Sometimes we might just be heading back up the mountain via Vilaflor on a long general ride with no efforts. That's pure cycling bliss. Normally, the rider who's been going best will have the short straw and be given the BoomBottle, also known as the Beats By Dre speaker. A playlist is selected, the remaining kilometres fly by to a motley selection from Dire Straits to Stereophonics via Eminem, and all is good in the world.

We arrived here once from the spring Classics and it was snowing as we landed at the airport. This is not what you expect in the Canaries, and you also don't expect an Austrian like Bernie Eisel to be unable to drive the hire car up the snowy climb to the hotel. Yet that's what happened.

I'd always believed that when driving in the snow you want to imagine you're grinding up the Mortirolo, high power but low torque. Bernie instead decided to slam his foot flat to the floor. The wheels were spinning so fast with so little traction that the speedo on the dashboard was reading 80mph. We were forced to abandon somewhere cold and lonely, stay the night in a random hotel and spend the hours of darkness fighting off an impromptu ant infestation. Cheers, Bernie.

I've also seen Chris Froome have a horrible crash going back down the other way. Front wheel puncture on a corner, tyre blowing out, a long slide down the road, a load of skin left behind him. But on most occasions, it's a climb as a treat. You don't need to put on a different sprocket; you can take it steady, if you're not a pro in training, and if you're carrying a little timber, it's not going to kill you.

It's a ride to enjoy, as a cycling tourist. Get that coffee and sarnie down you in Vilaflor, maybe treat yourself to a beer. You'll still get to 2000m, and you'll be rewarded with views and a dreamy descent.

Because Vilaflor, as a character, is the nice guy who gets on with everyone. He doesn't need to be the centre of attention, and not many have a bad word to say about him. He can be the main man, but he doesn't need to shout about it. He goes with the flow, Vilaflor.

Chirche

I refer to Solden in Austria as a bastard, for its length and steepness. In which case Chirche, which is steeper if not as long, is either a bas or a tard: the same evil character, just slightly less of it.

It's 3.5km. In a World Championship team pursuit final you could do that in 3 minutes and 16 seconds. On Chirche it takes 12 minutes, and that's if you're attacking it. Why? Because it's 11.6%. Except for the long stretches of 20% and over. I told you: it's a right tard.

I blame Tim Kerrison. He's an excellent coach, but he does take too much pleasure in hunting down brutal climbs for us on Tenerife. Life was simpler before Chirche. Life was more pleasant. My legs hurt less. Equally, I hadn't won the Tour de France. Kerrison 1–0 Thomas. But a tip, too: if you have the option, never take a Kerro shortcut. It's not always quicker, and it's always harder.

You don't stumble on Chirche. It doesn't stand out in Guia de Isora, the town at the bottom. You head up what looks like a normal side street, take a right-hander, a left-hander and you're away. Houses on either side, set into the hillside at an angle which makes you realize, if your quads haven't already sent back sufficient signals, that the road has started doing very strange things indeed.

You can't take much notice. You're too busy looking for any sign of the gradient shallowing off. You're going all in just to keep moving forward.

Another insider tip: there's the briefest of flat sections just before halfway, and the right line here is worth a few extra seconds if you're chasing a time on Strava. But otherwise, you have to pace yourself, because you'll be squeezing on the steeper parts, turn a corner waiting for it to calm down and then realize with a lurch that it's actually got steeper.

All the time Tim is behind in his hire car, the engine revving furiously, the smell of burning clutch filling the nostrils of those riders nearest to the rear. The closer he gets, the more we worry, as he's usually set us off at 15-second intervals, handicap style, quickest man starting last, so if he's making inroads, he's not alone.

It's easy to get carried away in this scenario and start chasing the man in front. But you have to resist the urge, because if you burn too many matches early on, you'll hit the really steep bit after six minutes and lose every one of those fifteen seconds in the space of 50 metres. Richie Porte was the king of these efforts and has the Strava records to prove it. Maybe just like in Willunga he'll receive the key to Chirche. Meanwhile, the car revs and the clutch burns and you wonder about setting up a

Tenerife-based clutch import business on your next visit, because every road is either up or down and no driver has any idea how to handle it.

It's not fancy, Chirche. You don't get many tourists making the trip. There isn't much vegetation, and there's quite an industrial feel to sections of it; big metal pipes above the ground, big water tanks next to the houses. There's a proper old-school Canarian feel to it. The old people look old. Most of the buildings don't look entirely finished. You begin to realize that there might not have been that much wealth in Tenerife before northern Europeans found out about the beaches.

But it's a great test of your form, a perfect way to gauge your legs compared to previous years, and it's a climb that makes sense in its own mad way, too. It goes somewhere – up to the top of Teide, joining the Bumpy climb after doing the same vertical distance in a quarter of the kilometres. There's a café at the top, with a nice view, and even nicer cold Coke Zero. There's even the occasional audience; we climbed it once at the same time as twenty schoolkids were standing outside, and they gave us a magnificent burst of cheering support, bringing an authentic Tour vibe to this desolate spot.

You need it. Even the last few minutes are twisty and super steep. You think you can see the finish, but a minute and a half later you're still grinding away, maxing out. We always have a thirty-six-tooth chainring on the front for Tenerife, and this is one of the major reasons why. You don't want to face Chirche with standard gearing. Not if you want to walk again at some point that week. There was talk at one stage of Luke Rowe attempting to big ring it, so to speak. The wager was that if he pulled it off, our South African mechanic, Gary Blem, would have to chop off his surfer dude locks. Both have backed down. So far.

It gets into your head, when you know it's coming up. No one in the team likes to be seen taking it seriously, but we all do. It starts the night before, when there's a noticeable change in the vibe around the dinner table – a prolonged silence, an absence of the usual larking. There's a nervous anticipation, a buzz over breakfast. By the time you're at the team car the following day, three of four big efforts done and Chirche in your sights, the box usually piled high with energy gels starts looking suspiciously empty. Riders are pedalling away with cheeks like hamsters and pockets like shoplifters. Everyone's already ditched their bottles – got to think about the extra weight – and then the bad acting begins.

'Ooops! I had no idea this was a double-espresso caffeine gel! I honestly thought it was an isotonic berry one. Maybe I'd better check another one, hold on. No, gutted, this one's caffeine too! Still, it's open now, eh?'

Chirche awaits, like one of the old boys who lives on its flanks. Short but hard, weathered but always there. A leathery face from sitting in the sun all day, a strange accent and a local dialect spoken only by him and his family. An old boy who welcomes you but in his own fierce way, with a homemade spirit based on plums he's picked from his garden, served as an aperitif, swallowed with a gasp and tears in your eyes.

That's Chirche. Every inch a bas.

Austria

Solden

Solden is a bastard. There's no other way to put it.

I've referred to it more specifically in the past as 'that big Swiss bastard', and meant it. Then I found out the confusing truth: it's actually in Austria. The problem came from the fact that they decided to include it in the Tour de Suisse, which must have been hard not to take as an insult if you're Swiss. 'What? We don't have enough mountains in Switzerland, so you had to go next door?'

I still should have noticed we'd crossed a national border, but that's the thing about Solden: you're in so much pain that the only thing you're capable of taking in is the distance between your front wheel and the rear wheel of the bloke in front.

Solden itself? A pretty Alpine town. I've got no problem with it at all. I've heard the coffee shops are good. They have to be, because if you're going 13.5 kilometres up a one-way road that claims to be the highest in Europe then you're going to need all the caffeine you can get. And even the name of that road sounds like an insult. Ötztaler Gletscherstrasse simply means the Ötztal glacier road. But said by a team's sporting director in a pre-stage briefing it's like being sworn at by an angry drunk.

Sometimes you're on the bus on the way to a stage, and you haven't done a recon ride of the decisive climb before, and you see its profile in the race book – the detailed route descriptions and maps that all the teams and commentators are given – and you think, no, that can't be right. Because they're not always right. An average gradient of 10.4%, a maximum of more than 16%? Nah. And then you see it coming down the valley, and you think, ah, it was right. Holy shit, this'll be some climb . . .

And that was my Solden debut, racing up it on stage five of the 2015 Tour de Suisse. And because I'm that way inclined, as we ticked off the kilometres on the way in, I was quite up for it. Of course, I was daunted, but I was also looking forward to it. How bad can this be? How well can I handle it?

Right, I thought. Don't overcook this at the start. And then I saw where the road was going and I thought, how can you undercook this? Because there is no easing in to Solden. It's straight up the valley. It has no pretences to be anything other than a bastard.

Jens Voigt, famous for telling his legs to shut up, had something else to say the day he got to the top of this one: 'Call mountain rescue!'

Solden is relentless. It's like a big heavyweight boxer, the biggest of the big. A massive puncher. If you leave your chin exposed, you're a goner. Knocked out, no coming back.

It starts on the run-in, a nervousness in the peloton. It's quite draggy, and it means the race is always on, even before the climb has properly begun, because everyone's thinking they need a decent position as the road kicks up.

That's what you'd ordinarily do before a big climb. But this is so long that the normal rules go out the back. You're going to be climbing for an hour. There is no rush. Whether you're in twentieth place or fortieth there is time for all of it to work itself out. Be patient, gird your loins, check your pockets for energy gels and Haribo.

It's not just the steepness of the road that's upsetting. It's how straight it is. There are hairpins on the road, and signs counting them down, just as there are on Alpe d'Huez and the Stelvio. But whereas there are twenty-one of them on the Alpe and almost fifty on Stelvio, so they come at you fast and you can tick them off, use them to drag you up, there are fewer than ten on Solden. They're both there and never there. You pass one and it's so long before the next that you start to doubt you ever passed one in the first place. You're in some sort of hairpin purgatory, lost in the long joyless wait in between.

You begin in the forest. You stay in there for what seems like a lifetime. You are grateful for the shade, in the way you would be thankful for a gum-shield against that heavyweight; it's not going to save you, but it might make the fight ever so slightly less painful. Then you think it's over, and you're wrong. You're not even halfway.

Halfway is a series of toll booths spread out across the road, because you can ski all year round on the glaciers at the top and this road goes nowhere else, so you're only going up it if you really want to and are prepared to pay for the privilege.

The tolls are the only part where you're offered any sort of respite. There's a short section as the road widens out where it even goes slightly downhill. It doesn't last, and it actually freaks you out a little. It's designed for a decent number of cars, but now it's deserted, as if you're on a ride during the lockdown part of the coronavirus pandemic, or the toll road leads you to a land where the apocalypse has wiped out all humankind except for a bunch of thin, suffering men who all weigh less than 70kg.

The road surface is a dream. It always is in Austria and Switzerland, in Germany, even up high when the freezing and expanding of any water on the tarmac should break it up like a stale biscuit. But that's the only crumb of comfort to be taken. It's hard to keep the mind strong at this point. They talk in pro racing about the most important two inches of your body being the top ones. When you're in trouble at the bottom, tell yourself everyone's in trouble. Tell yourself you're pushing the guy just in front, scaring him, not hanging on, waiting to be dropped.

Bad thoughts try to take hold as you pass the booths, all their barriers up. I'm buying my ticket now. No turning back. It's just going to be pain from here, all the way up to the race finish at almost 2800 metres. You tell yourself that it flattens off slightly three kilometres out. You answer yourself by saying that three kilometres out is still miles away up there, and that a slight flattening will make no difference when it then kicks back up to 11%, you've been riding uphill for an hour and your legs have had everything useful sucked out of them.

And it's the altitude too that gets you, that saps you the closer to the finish you get. I'm lucky. I seem naturally built to cope with the ordinary challenges that altitude brings, at least compared to my fellow low-lying Europeans. I'm not claiming to have any long-lost Colombian ancestry. Maybe it comes down to having been brought up in the northern Cardiff suburbs at 39 metres above sea level. But this is not ordinary altitude. The top of Alpe d'Huez, or at least the part we climb to, is 1800m. Another 1000 vertical metres on top of that makes a mess of even the best-laid plans.

Any sort of acceleration blows you apart. What would be an easy effort back down the mountain becomes maximal. Your red zone – the point where you're pushing so hard that things start going wrong fast – shifts dramatically. On Alpe d'Huez you might not want to push beyond 500 watts of power. On the upper half of Solden, that'll drop to 350 watts. It takes the same out of you and you get far less in return, but you have to get your head around these new limits. If you haven't experienced this sort of altitude before, if you're just looking down at the computer on your handlebar stem and working off your normal power zones, you're fighting to hold something which is no longer real. And it is not going to end well.

Here's another perplexing thing about Solden. It can actually be tougher trying to cruise up it rather than racing on your limits. When you're close to the front, when you're battling for a podium place in the general classification, there is a pinpoint focus to all that you're doing. The pain almost makes sense. It has a purpose and a clear reward. You can kid yourself that the brutality of it is passing by under your wheels. 'Okay, we've gone through the hardest section, the easy part's almost here . . .' The fact that the easy bit is still 7% and is gone before you can even notice doesn't matter. You're doing well. You're doing much better than almost everything else. It's pain as a virtue and pleasure.

When you're just surviving – well, all you can think about is surviving. In the grupetto, the last bunch of riders on the road, you have so much less to distract you from those thoughts. You know you're doing badly – everyone else is up ahead. You look left and right and you see the suffering and you can hear it too. 'Right. I'm riding up to a dead end, where I'll turn around and come back down. All that, for this . . .'

You have to fuel it right on Solden to have any chance. It's a climb to make sure a couple of the gels in your jersey pocket are caffeine ones. You'll feel the kick when they go down. But you can overdo it, because at that sort of altitude, too much can end up going to your head rather than your legs. You can feel lightheaded, and not in the happy, giddy sense. Ideally, you'd want to eat something, since the effort is such a long one. But try getting something solid down you when you're sucking in air like a free diver coming up from the depths and you'll inhale it rather than swallow. You'll choke. So gels it is. And you take them on a kilometres-to-go basis rather than ride time. One at the bottom. Another after 3km, another after 6km. If you have extras in your pocket, you'll make sure you use them all up. If they're not caffeinated, they'll help your head; sometimes it's just that sweetness in your mouth that makes you feel better, giving you a Pavlovian energy boost.

If you know there's only 4km to go and you find two, it's a 'sod it' moment. In for a penny. There have been times when I've even triple-gelled – tearing the tops off with my teeth; squeezing from the hand, rather than sucking; deep breath, swallow, a couple more deep breaths, second swallow, then back to focusing on my breathing and holding the wheel in front. There's none of the careful extraction of every last drop that there is if you're on a training ride and miles from home. It's one of the small luxury perks of having a job that requires you to put yourself through this: no one is going to complain about you using too many sponsored gels.

Mountains bring their own weather systems. The top of big mountains bring anything they like. Snow in June. Blistering heat a week later. Rain, often from nowhere in what was otherwise a pleasant, sunny day. Solden's cold, but because of what you're doing to get up it, you tend not to notice until you stop. A heart rate of 180 beats per minute makes your eyes water, but all that blood being rushed out through your capillaries does keep you toasty. It's only as you cross the line that you realize your jersey is soaked, and only as you freewheel towards the team bus with your soigneur's hand in the small of your back that you first feel the bite. It's a climb to have a long-sleeved jersey draped over your shoulders as soon as you finish, to pull leg-warmers on, to think about a cheeky woolly hat if you're solo and waiting for your mates.

That stage in 2015 was, for me, like a deep immersion in everything Solden can do to a rider. I was sitting second in the GC, and I understood what a pivotal day this was. Lose it on Solden and you can freefall out of the top ten, let alone off the podium. And so coming into the climb we were all on the pedals, all pushing hard before the part where we were supposed to be pushing hard, all close to 400 watts just to hold on.

Riders were doing crazy things. The American Joe Dombrowski launched an attack right at the bottom. Mate, what are you doing? No one gets away there. No one can hold it for that long. Simon Špilak had a pop before we'd reached the tolls. Same result – brief period of freedom and fame, soon swallowed back up. Domenico Pozzovivo went. And came back.

You have to play dull and sensible rather than brave and doomed. I had Sergio Henao with me, and a Colombian teammate is exactly what you want when battling that sort of gradient and altitude. All the jumping around at the front – had I tried following those boys at that sort of altitude, I would have ended up in hospital. So when Thibaut Pinot attacked too, I let him go – not abandoning hope, not sitting up, but rationing what I had left. Tom Dumoulin was doing the same: dropped from the lead group early, but only because he was time-trialling his effort up it, holding his power at the optimum level rather than spiking into the red and then crashing back down. Dumoulin knows what he's doing in that situation. Ride tempo, not a rollercoaster. Other riders on their own for 8km might crack and lose much more. Tom is the epitome of someone who lets go to sit in a safer place.

On Alpe d'Huez you have the fans to keep you going. In the Pyrenees the same. The Basques might even be the best supporters of all. On the Tour de Suisse they're thinner on the ground, which is a shame, partly because us riders need them, partly because Solden is almost perfect for watching elite racing. Now the lack of hairpins works; you can see riders coming up the valley and you can see them going away. The road's wide, so you can park your car or pitch your tent; we will not be going fast, so you can stare into our eyes and understand the beautiful misery we're going through.

The smaller numbers also mean a rider will hear everything you shout at them. There's no getting lost in the hubbub. There's no giant sound system set up by a load of Dutchmen with their faces and bodies painted orange. And so you can find yourself in quite an intimate internal dialogue with a German-speaking spectator who has grammatically perfect English, just delivered in an unintentionally abrupt manner.

'Geraint! Geraint!'

'Yes, that's me.'

'Come on! What are you doing?'

Eh? I'm doing fine. I'm up near the front.

'You should be leading!'

Mate, I'm doing okay; I'm letting them get away but maintaining my pace.

'What are you doing?'

It's called riding tempo. Where's Dombrowski now, eh? Eh?

Sure enough, we kept coming back. I found myself on the wheel of Miguel Ángel López, and being within croaking distance of another Colombian mountain goat was another proper boost. Being Colombian he insisted on riding a Colombian way, accelerating on the steep bits, appearing to be giving me a proper kicking, but even Colombians can't maintain repeated digs like that near the top of Solden. So he kept coming back to me, and my internal monologue switched focus from direct fan to rival: 'Come on mate, if we properly time-trialled this together, we could get a load of time back on Pinot. Why the flashy moves?'

We finished together, only a few seconds down on Špilak and Pozzovivo, only forty-odd down on Pinot. And I limped away from my debut brush with Solden with something almost priceless in my pocket: the knowledge that I was climbing better than ever before, that I could hold my own in the high mountains in a way that could maybe make me a regular in the upper reaches of a stage-race GC.

Weight matters on the big monster climbs. That's what I was learning. You'll hear a lot of technical stuff about power-to-weight ratios in cycling, but it's how it feels when the road goes up and up that matters most to a rider.

I was still gradually working out that my ideal weight for a stage race through the mountains is 68kg. I'd been a track rider and big, by the standards of the pro peloton. I'd been a Classics rider, more about power in short bursts than sustaining climbing. And although there are only 2 kilograms between 71kg and 69kg, you drop that and it's transformational. That drop – it's like losing four full water bottles from your jersey pockets. Imagine how stretched a jersey would look loaded down with four bidons. If you took it off, it would be dragging along the floor.

In racing terms? If you can maintain the same power and lose those 2kg, you go from minutes behind and focused on just getting to the finish to the front group on the road. That's the easy bit. Drop your weight, keep your power. Sounds simple, hey? The hard part is actually getting there. If I were a good club rider with a day job doing something else but watching what I ate and training and racing hard, my weight would probably be 72/73kg. To get down to 68kg, which is the sweet spot between losing enough weight to fly but not enough to crash, I have to get used to being hungry. All the time. Hungry means tired. Hungry can mean moody.

It's not just volume of food. You still need to understand what, when and why you are or aren't eating something. It's what you eat and when you eat it that makes the difference: balancing the carbs and the protein, because you still need to train hard to keep that power; riding on empty sometimes to teach your body to burn fat as a fuel, too. After all these years I can get down to 70kg okay now. I'll start back training in November after a good blowout. I'll be in the high 70s. By March, I'm closer to 70kg on the nose. But the last little bit is so difficult and takes so long: 70 to 69kg is horrible; 69 to 68kg is brutal. It'll take me until mid-May or early June to get down there, and then I'm hanging on for the start of the

Tour de France. Once I'm racing, because of how much fuel I need to take on to get through stage after punishing stage, it's creeping back up again.

Solden helped to teach me all this. In 2015, I was light and feeling quick. A year later I came back to the same climb in the same race and lost just a fraction too much. I was down to 67kg, and that single kilogram finished me off. I spent the whole week battling round feeling empty. I learned, and I took the lessons to the Tour in 2018. It's better to be 69kg and strong than 67 and empty.

Thank you, Solden. For some things at least, you big bastard.

Italy

Cipressa and Poggio

Some climbs, you ride them and you just know. They make sense. They dominate the landscape, look like nothing else, ride like nothing else. You can't miss them and you can never forget them.

The Cipressa and Poggio? You have to find them, get off the main drag, take the correct little turn. When you do, among the olive trees and Mediterranean pines and cypress trees, you start pedalling and think: this is okay. It's pleasant. This is easy. And you go over the summits before you've ever had to get out of the saddle, and you coast down the other side, and stop for a coffee in San Remo itself, and you look back at where you came from, and wonder, was that it?

The Cipressa. Five and a half kilometres at an average gradient of 4.1%. The tiniest ramp of 9%. Ten minutes racing and it's done. The Poggio: shorter and shallower still, 4km at an average of 3.7%.

They don't matter. Until they do. When they mean everything.

It's not about what the Cipressa and Poggio are. It's where they come. When you hit the first after 270km of racing, and the summit of the second is 5.4km from the finish line – that's why they're iconic. That's why elite riders love them, and that's why they're revered by fans. All that comes before, the six hours or so of racing, is just an aperitif – an aperitif in a long glass, possibly with ice, but one that leaves you slower, with your energy gone and your mind befuddled.

Of course, you can just tootle up the Cipressa and Poggio in training or on a recon. But when you've ridden from Milan, and you're on your limit, and one of the great one-day prizes is dancing just out of reach – then they're hard. It's like the back nine at St Andrews. Stick a top 100 golfer on there on an ordinary day and they'll stroll it. But after three and a half days of cut and thrust, with a huge crowd in and television cameras everywhere, strong men fall apart.

Let's put this another way, a British angle on a quintessentially Italian occasion. If you decided to pop to the kebab shop at lunchtime in the middle of a standard working day, your doner and chips would be underwhelming at best. Why am I having this? I'd much rather be eating something else. But go to the same kebab shop and order the same doner and chips at 2am after a spectacular all-day session and it's the greatest meal in the world. Every mouthful is amazing. The only drawback is that it's finite. And you're loving it so much you don't want it to end.

That's the Cipressa and Poggio. Draped in history, the killer final act in a five-part drama, the final session of a five-day Test match.

The part you don't see, sometimes, is what takes it out of your legs on the way: the battle over the Passo del Turchino, how technical the descent to the coast can be if the weather's bad. In 2013, the snow was so heavy over the top that we couldn't make it through. The organizers must have known at the start – if it's raining heavily in Milan, it's snowing on the Turchino – but they still sent us off, and then bussed us all down to the coast to restart it, all of us half-destroyed, frantically searching for dry clothes, for cups of tea, for anything to bring us back to life. Ian Stannard was so cold he was almost in tears. After that, the Cipressa and Poggio felt like the Télégraphe and Galibier.

In a more normal Milan–San Remo the race is full-on along the Ligurian coast, although you never get that sense watching on TV, and a frantic chase up and down the three little hills that follow – the Capo Mele, Capo Cervo and Capo Berta. There's jostling, there's fighting. You can feel the tension creeping in, the anger, the tiredness. Now you have to concentrate all the way. There are fans hanging off balconies, flares burning in your peripheral vision, smoke blurring your eyes and choking your lungs.

And then the Cipressa is there: the yellow-painted houses, the reddish-brown tiled roofs, the old church tower. There's a slight descent into a corner, a gradual bend round to the right and then a skate across the black and white paint of a zebra crossing. I've crashed there before. When it's damp that sort of paint is slippery as ice. Someone braked hard and late in front of me, I touched my brakes and was straight down. Race over, no coming back, not there.

So you want to be top thirty there, top forty maximum. The climb begins and it's solid and draggy, but the speeds are intense. The race for the top is to be in a good position for the descent rather than for the summit itself; there'll be one or two attacks, but it's rare that anyone who goes away on the Cipressa stays away all the way to San Remo, because you're still 22km from the finish.

Pedalling hard on the way down, straight back to the road you've just left, and a barrel along there for 10km or so. On your recon ride it seems to go on for ever, a drawn-out pause in the experience. In the race it's on fast-forward. It's over before you know. And you could miss the turn-off for the Poggio if you weren't chasing a load of multi-coloured jerseys in front and a pair of camera motorbikes out beyond them, because it's so inconspicuous. You just bear right off the main road and the road narrows and it's game on.

You're in it, and you're fighting all the time. That's what throws you. You're consistently on the pedals hard. You press and press. When the attacks begin on the Poggio and it all kicks off, and they're going off all the way to the top, you have to close any gap that appears in front of you. It's like when you're riding on Zwift and it tells you to close a 2-metre gap or be in the wind and feel the resistance change immediately. You sprint to hold the wheel in front; you sprint out of the corners if you're in the lead. You glance down at your power meter and the watts are pouring out of you.

All of us in the front group, we all know where the real dangerous moves are going to come. The first couple of kilometres are solid, then it flattens out, then it kicks up again. That's where you launch. Go on the second steep part, lose your pursuers in the twists of the road that follow. Vincenzo Nibali did it in 2018; he had tried it with Fabian Cancellara and Simon Gerrans six years earlier, and it had worked again, only for Simon to do the other two in a sprint at the death. Paulo Bettini's done it. Laurent Jalabert's done it, too.

It's a pure moment, the couple of seconds when an attack comes. If you've had your caffeine, if you're ready for it, you're up for that twitch in a rival's calf muscles and their sudden jump out of the saddle. When you're in form, the big moves seem to happen in slow motion. You see them coming and you have all the time in the world to respond. It's like you're Spiderman and all your Spider senses are pinging. You're aware of your breathing; you're aware of where everyone else is around you. When you're suffering, it happens too fast. You can't react. But if you are able to respond when a Peter Sagan or Julian Alaphilippe goes, it's one of the best feelings in the world, because you know how good they are at it. When it's you doing the attacking, it should be instinctive. You might have a plan in your head – I'm going to launch somewhere in the next 500 metres – but it's something unconscious that tells you exactly when. Yep – this feels right; let's whack it.

I've tried something different to the Nibali model myself, and it didn't quite work. In 2015, I went away with BMC's Daniel Oss between the Cipressa and Poggio, then used him as long as I could on the Poggio, thinking I would attack in the usual place. But I should have gone earlier. We had a seventeen-second gap at the bottom of the climb, but that wasn't big enough. To stand any chance I should instead have gone full gas from the bottom. By the time I went solo, I still managed to build up a cushion of about twelve seconds, but then I looked back and saw Luca Paolini riding flat out for Alexander Kristoff. Too late. I held a little advantage until about 50 metres from the top, and the big hitters swamped me from behind and I was just another piece of jetsam back in the group. Race over again. Different way, same result.

I've made Milan-San Remo sound predictable. It's anything but. It's the race where anything can happen, and the Cipressa and Poggio jab-jab combo is why. A GC guy like Nibali can win it. It can be a Classics rider like Michał Kwiatkowski or Julian Alaphilippe. It can be a pure sprinter like Mark Cavendish or Caleb Ewan.

And so much of it is what happens on the back side of those climbs. I could write a chapter just on the descents, on where you need to be and what you have to do. They are lovely to ride, but you fly down them on a knife edge. There is no resting, never a hope of coasting. There are corners tight enough that you can either hold a gap or lose one; there are corners where you either come horribly close to crashing, yet keep it up and race away on exhilaration, or lean it that fraction too far and come clattering down.

There's always a lot of talk about who rides those descents the best. It's different in the dry and in the wet; it matters if you're out front or in a group. There are corners that tighten up on you and catch you out if you haven't been paying attention on your recon, and there are a few where you can stay off the brakes entirely if you've got the guts for it. Nibali gets the love for how he came down the Poggio, but the majority of top riders would have matched his pace had they been on the front riding solo, too. On your own, you can pick the best line, brake when you want to brake, not when the rider in front does. You can sprint out of those corners because there's no one in your way. In the chase group, a rider from a rival team swings over, his work done, and you're swerving to get round him. Someone else gets twitchy on their brakes, you have to pull harder to not go into the back of them. You can lose two or three seconds every time, and the solo escape stays solo and stays away. If you're a great descender, maybe you can get away with it. You think about Cav in 2009, working his way up the Cipressa on George Hincapie's wheel, plenty of Columbia-High Road teammates with him. Cav's a great descender when he knows what's on the line. He was content with the knowledge that it might be crash or win. And once they set him up so well, he was always going to be fastest in the finale, even if poor Heinrich Haussler did briefly think he might hang on out front.

Cav got it right on the Cipressa and Poggio. If you want to win Milan-San Remo, you cannot get it wrong.

The Stelvio

The Tour de France has Alpe d'Huez. The Giro d'Italia has the Stelvio. That's how it works, this road that looks like a strawberry bootlace pulled out of the packet, all bent back on itself and going on, and on and on.

More than twenty-four kilometres of going on, if you come from the usual side at Ponte di Stelvio. Cyclists want to conquer it. Car fans want to drive it. *Top Gear* probably want to do it again. Because most people do, once they've had a bite.

You genuinely look forward to the Stelvio, as a rider. Yes, it's a brute. Yes, you will suffer on it. But so much has happened up there, so many Giros won and lost, so many reputations made or blown away. None of us would want to finish our pro careers without having danced up those hairpins. We'd feel incomplete.

In the same way that the best club rides aren't the easy ones where the weather is mild and the route pleasant, the punishment dished out by the Stelvio is the secret to its allure. The club rides you're still talking about in ten years' time are the ones where you took a wrong turn on the way back, ran out of food, ran out of money, got caught in a snowstorm and broke your front derailleur so that you had to time-trial 20 miles home with the big ring on and no feeling in your hands. So it is with elite races: the time you got blown off your bike by a gale at Gent-Wevelgem, when Milan-San Remo got stopped by snow on the Turchino Pass, the time rain turned Strade Bianche into a mess of mud and puddles and muddy crashes into puddles. It's the sense of delayed enjoyment: God, this is horrible right now, but it's going to be amazing when I'm home and warm and giving it large to everyone who didn't make it. It's why you find yourself secretly hoping for a wet day at Paris-Roubaix, unless you're in the nowhere-lands of fifteenth to thirtieth, where it'll get rid of a few rivals but not enough. The more challenging a race or a stage, the more you love it, secretly. We're all masochists deep down, us cyclists. We love a moan, but we love what causes the moan even more.

Race organizers sort of understand this and sort of don't. They assume the way to make racing more exciting is to make everything harder. Steeper climbs, more climbs. You get race profiles that look like a hair comb. But too much of it, too forced, ends up neutralizing it. It doesn't feel real. It doesn't feel natural.

The Stelvio? You can't fake the Stelvio. And no matter how familiar it is to you – how easily you can picture that pale grey road zig-zagging up the bare mountainside, climbing this way and then back and disappearing up into the clouds – it's always a strange sort of pleasure to see it again. You race in Belgium and relish the cobbles and the bergs. You do Gent-Wevelgem in tights and a long-sleeved jersey and the rain; you hammer it round Flanders in April, fighting the wind, springing up 500-metre climbs. And then the next month, you're inching your way up an endless epic in Italy, forty-five minutes behind the stage winner, and it's the same sport. Unrecognizable landscape, contrasting personal role, totally different physical challenge. But the same sport, and pretty much the same machine between you and the road: still pedals, still a chain, still wheels the same circumference. You don't get that in rugby. You don't get that in football.

And it's the climb that makes it. For us, these mountain passes, even more so than the one-day Monuments – these are our iconic stadiums. These are our Wembleys and Maracanas. It's where you want to be, where your career has to go. It's the heroes that have gone before and the epics that have played out. And they can take you anywhere: to the depths of misery when it's lashing down with freezing Alpine rain, to a strange giddy place when you're riding them as the final climb in a three-week stage race that feels like the last day of exams in school – when you know all that work is done, you've all made it through and you're about to let it go in a way you haven't been able to for months.

And the Stelvio has grace, too: forty-eight hairpins, an average gradient of 7.4%, only briefly above 9%. While the Mortirolo is all brute force, the Stelvio is older, more stylish. It feels more French Alps than Italian, the road wide and its surface dreamy. You see the drone shots taken during races, picking out riders sprinkled down the valley, and it's misery as a form of art. You can be mates with the Stelvio, and you can never be mates with the Mortirolo. If the Stelvio's in a bad mood you certainly keep your head down. Anything that stands 2750m tall carries crazy latent menace. He can be a nightmare to be around, when he wants to be. But he'll look after you, too, the charismatic old charmer. He'll give you days out you'll never forget.

To the racing. You've got multiple options to attack here, not least because the climb is so long. Any attack could look great for a minute and yet be meaningless 2km or twenty minutes later. If you can, it's better to play the waiting game. Let others lose their nerve. Let them have the motorbikes and helicopters chasing them up the road. Stay invisible until the point it really matters, then throw off your cloak and go hard.

Understand what hard is. If you're on the front of a group, you can find a nice rhythm on the Stelvio. As you get higher, you need to stay smart. It's like the Col du Portet; the higher you go, the more sneaky the effects of altitude. Lower down you might be expecting to push 400 or 420 watts. The same perceived effort at the top will only produce 360. So don't go chasing it, and never panic. If you're going to attack, anything over 700 watts is going to blow your doors off. The more times you go into the red when you're that high, the more dangerous it is for you, not your rivals. If you want to attack, chuck in a little surge, get a gap and then settle down. It's like going out on the town as a teenager: love where you are, but understand your limit, even if not many others do.

And use your team. If you're a GC contender, the absolute minimum number of teammates you need with you at the bottom of the Stelvio is two. Even then, they're going to have to turn themselves inside out for you. If you can get one to do a Jonathan Castroviejo and ride hard for you for 10km, then you've won the Stelvio lottery. Either way, keep them with you for as long as possible. It's worse being on your own on this mountain than the Mortirolo because it's possible to ride faster; you haven't all been instantly reduced to dust. Drafting doesn't help on the Mortirolo. You're going too slow. On the Stelvio, by contrast, you can get quite the benefit, particularly if there's a headwind coming down the valley. It can be the difference between riding at 300 watts and 400.

If they can ride a decent tempo, they'll kill off several attacks before they're even launched. You can send them back to the team car to get you food and drinks, or just nick theirs if it's getting a bit squeaky. Once you're at 5km to go, climbing up above 2400m, it's every man for himself. But you'll have more of yourself left if your teammates have used themselves up for you getting to that point.

Either way, you have to pace it. It's like riding a flat 25-mile time-trial: you can go hard all the way, and if you're blowing at the end, it doesn't matter; if you're blowing with 5 miles to go, however, it's game over. And when you blow 2000m up the Stelvio, it's even worse. It's not air hissing out. It's an explosion.

Build into it. If you were making yourself a playlist for this climb, you'd have to structure it like a wedding. It can't be banging at the bottom. Don't waste 'Sweet Caroline' for when the guests are still enjoying a coffee. Hold it back until the dancefloor is busy. Only deploy 'Delilah' when everyone is arm in arm and the men have their ties around their foreheads like Rambo. You start with Tom Jones and there's only one way it can end: messy.

Ordinarily, riding for that time while drinking as much as you need to, you'd need to stop for a call of nature. But there's no peeing on the Stelvio because you're working too hard. You're sweating everything out. The greater challenge is keeping your concentration for that long. Your mind can wander. Should Arsenal sign another central defender? How many caps could Alun Wyn Jones conceivably end up with? What on earth am I going to get Sa for her next birthday? Then you suddenly snap back into focus, look down at your power meter and realize you're going fractionally slower than you could be. And fractionally, in grand tours, is the difference between podium and forgotten. Come on, I'm on the Stelvio here. This is my time. Not Mikel Arteta's.

Your nutrition strategy is all about keeping going. Riding uphill for an hour will empty anyone's tank. If you've done the Mortirolo earlier in the day, as you generally have in the Giro, you'll be weary whether you're in grupetto or front group. You're also close to the end of the stage, so you can get some sugar down you in a morale-boosting way without fearing the effects of a spike and crash. Haribos always go down a treat, particularly after three weeks of a tour when you've had the same energy bars day after day. For the same reason, the Stelvio also sees significant levels of swapping between teams. Ooh, that baked apple gel looks nice, is it as moreish as the morello cherry one?

This is the nice thing about the grupetto: everyone looking out for one another, while up front all they want to do is drop each other, the savages. At least, that is, until all that band-of-brothers camaraderie gets lobbed out of the window twenty-four hours later, when you're all sprinting for the line in Milan. But for now, the normal rules don't apply. You'll throw anything down your neck. Up front your leader is taking gels on a scientific basis. You're taking them whenever you find one.

I was chatting once with Adam Hansen in the grupetto up the Stelvio, both of us nearly on empty, both dreaming of what we were going to eat and drink once the horror was all over. Adam's the great survivor. He rode twenty consecutive Grand Tours. He knows what it takes. And so when he was handed a beer by a spectator on the side of the road with 10km still to go, I took pity on him.

'Oh, why would he do that to you, mate? That's really rubbing it in. Want me to go to the team car to open it for you?'

Look, I did fancy a sneaky taste. But Adam was insistent. 'Nah, you're okay mate. Crack on.'

We crossed the line forty-five minutes later, broken. And Adam rolled up alongside me, saying, 'Here you go, mate,' and handed me the beer. 'You carried that all the way up here just for me?' I was almost in tears. And while the beer wasn't the optimum temperature, it was cold enough at the top to make it one of the greatest beverages I have ever drunk in my life.

The other great joy, and one less illicit, is a bidon filled with hot tea that comes back from the team car via a teammate. You need to get it down you quick, because at that altitude it's going tepid faster than we're going uphill, but for the brief few moments when your mouth is full of strong, sugary tea, you're as happy as any rider can be: on one of the great climbs, towards the top, only a Sunday procession to come before the post-race parties, drinking a beverage that is causing everyone around to stare at you with enormous jealousy. As well as taking you back to Sunday afternoon round at your nan's.

The temperature of the tea matters because the cold bites on the Stelvio. If it's clear and chilly, that's ideal; you're working so hard you don't notice. If it snows, that's still sort of okay, because snow is dry. You can brush it off. It's a cold rain that you dread the most. It's 3 degrees and you're soaked and you're sending people back to the team car to get extra kit, but when you stop to pull it on you find you don't have the legs to chase back on. Your teammates will try to help, but their fingers have gone numb, too, and now there are two people trying to get a glove on one person's wet hand, and that never works out well. The gloves have a lining. You've got two fingers stuck in one hole, so you pull them out, and the whole lining reverses, and you're frantically shoving your hand into what appears to be a glove with no fingers. The team doctor jumps out of the team car to help – not because he's an expert in gloves, but because he's neither driving nor speaking on the radio to more sensible riders. You're cold, hungry and tired. He's had an excellent formal education and a number of prospective career paths and is wondering how it's come to standing on the side of a mountain in the pouring rain swearing at a glove.

Dream scenario? You find out your swanny is a kilometre up the road with extra kit and tea. You're too cold to talk. They dress you like a mother would a newborn. Fresh warm hat. Fresh dry rain jacket, new dry gloves. A push and chase back into the grupetto, the chase helping to warm you up further. You feel a million dollars. A life of small pleasures.

There is always snow somewhere, on the Stelvio. It's a hard climb to recon as it only really opens properly just before the Giro, and there are often big banks of snow pushed to the side as you climb – dirty, end-of-season snow, full of strange black bits and stone; snow you can't ever imagine thawing, even in August. But it's beautiful, all the same, whenever you're up there. You just have to accept the view you have. If you're riding well and you're towards the front, you can look back down the strawberry bootlace and see riders strung out all the way down it. And if you're in the grupetto, you can look up and see groups up ahead that appear quite close, but are actually 3km and ten minutes away because of the switchbacks. You can see the top of the climb and get there and then realize that it's not the top at all. It might not even be the beginning of the top. Hopefully, it's the end of the middle, but the Stelvio is so long and twisty you can never be entirely sure.

I've seen things I'll never forget on that mountain. Thomas de Gendt, winning the stage, bagging third place in the Giro as a result. Afterwards he said all he wanted for tea was sausages, having given them up to shed weight. His nickname in the peloton is now Sausages. You're not in an imaginative mood when you've finished the Stelvio.

And I've seen my friend Mark Cavendish by the finish area at the top, waiting to discover if he'd held on to the

Giro's points jersey from Joaquim Rodríguez, who needed fourth place or better to nick it on the penultimate day. And then the updated standings coming through, and Rodríguez being ahead by a single point after twenty days of racing, and Cav crying his eyes out in a lonely hotel room, suddenly just a kid from the Isle of Man rather than the swaggering sprinter everyone thinks he is. Those images haunt my memory of that climb.

But that's the thing about the Stelvio. Always memories, always something to take with you across the world, beautiful or bad or somewhere in between.

The Mortirolo

Oh no. Not the Mortirolo.

There's a trio of brutes in this book. Solden, the big Swiss, sorry, Austrian bastard. The Portet, two horrible climbs in one. And the Mortirolo, a road that makes no sense. That's your rogues' gallery, your podium of pain, a triptych that's a curse for those who choose to take them on.

I think the middle section is the worst. The first third is horrible, but you're mentally fresh. You feel ready to tackle it. The middle third, you start getting slapped round the chops by repeated ramps of 14%, 16%, 18%. That's ridiculous. Other climbs might throw one of those in, but then back off apologetically. This one continues to elbow you in the face. You inch your way round one of the innumerable corners – corners that don't even count as one of the official thirty-nine hairpins – and you expect a little respite, because this sort of madness can't carry on, and then the next section swings into view through the trees, and you think: oh. It does go on. And it's getting worse. Oh.

There are points on the Mortirolo when you wonder if it's ever going to end. You've been climbing so slowly that your Garmin has auto-paused, assuming that you've stopped. Let's scratch this from the official record: it doesn't actually count as moving. And yet you still have six kilometres of the 12.5km to go, and the average gradient is never going to drop below 10.5% and there'll be nothing for you to look at except those oppressive trees and this thin, single-track sliver of tarmac glistening in the damp and rising up in front of you like a spitting cobra.

Idle thoughts float into your mind. How was it possible to build this road? Why didn't the wet tarmac just fall off the mountain? How did the workmen stand up straight?

As the pain gets worse, your mental picture gets bleaker with it. The trees are dark green. The road is dark grey. The clouds are usually low and heavy. It's claustrophobic and gloomy and repressive. There's nothing at the top of this climb – no village, no cathedral, no ski resort. It's a pointless ascent, a road to nowhere, a stairway to hell. Golf, like cycling, uses the natural environment all around it to enhance its pleasures: a green tucked between natural mounds, a tee on a cliff top, a fairway wound around a stream. A lot of time great cycling climbs do that, too – taking you along a spectacular valley, showing you a view that would take your breath away had you got any spare, lifting you to heights that you could otherwise never reach. The Mortirolo? It shows you nothing but the dark corners of your soul. You climb it, you descend on to the same valley road you came off to go up it. There are no views in that forest, nothing pretty. You may as well be riding in a tunnel. It's just screaming fans and frantic scribbles on the road.

You never walk down a fairway of a top course and think, why is there a hole here? On the Mortirolo you pedal and you pedal and the question gets splintered off into a singular sharp point: why?

If the Mortirolo were human, it would still barely be human. It would be a child raised by wolves. It would be a man who even now cannot communicate without also trying to fight you. You don't just not want to get on the wrong side of him, you don't want to see him at all. He has no friends. He scares the local Mafia. Even villains have one redeeming feature – a kindness to their grandmother, a love of retired greyhounds. The Mortirolo has none. The Mortirolo makes the Stelvio seem like an afternoon in a sunny pub beer garden.

Look, maybe I'm bitter. I've raced up it twice, both times in the Giro d'Italia; once as a heavy-boned youngster with Barloworld in 2008 and again with Sky in 2012. On each occasion I was in the grupetto, the last bunch on the road. Maybe it would be different if I went back now, as someone who has worked out how to climb and how to turn down chips. But I'm not sure. Back in the day, I was nervous taking on any climb in the World Tour. That's gone, but the menace of the Mortirolo remains. For everyone.

The road is so heavy. And in case the combination of

gradient and rough surface wasn't slowing you down enough, they've then stuck in a series of drains running horizontally across your path. You're not going fast enough to bunny-hop them; you'd have to be in the air for thirty seconds at that pace. You bump down into them and you throw away another precious slice of energy bumping out of them again.

It's very rare you change your gearing as a pro rider these days. But the Mortirolo *is* very rare. And so the sensible team mechanic will stick a proper mountain-bike gear on there for you – a thirty-six on the front and maybe a thirty or thirty-two on the back. It's not to help you win the stage, it's to get you up it. It's to help with the nerves. You can see it in the TV motorbikes ahead of you; they're having to weave across the road to maintain enough momentum to keep moving forward.

It's the same reason why there's very little chat with riders around you as you climb. You don't want to talk. If you feel you can, you keep it to yourself. Open a conversation with a man suffering next to you and he can see it as an insult. Oh, rubbing it in, are we? If you've got so much breath, why aren't you further up the mountain?

The make-up of the grupetto is a strange one on something like the Mortirolo. You get the usual guys, the mainstays, always there and always knowing how to ride it, how to calculate to the minute how slow they can go to conserve as much energy as possible. Why ride up a climb at 320 watts if 300 watts gets you inside the time cut? Slow on the climbs, fast on the descents and flat. You can't beat a big twenty-up chain-gang through and off in the valley.

But then you get some guys having an easy time, saving themselves for the breakaway stage the next day. They're quite capable of finishing the stage a good twenty minutes earlier, but they don't want to. They want to save their legs. And so while they know the way the grupetto works, they also can't help themselves. Suddenly, they're at the front, pressing on, half-wheeling the guy they're next to and getting a fitting reaction.

'Whooah! Piiiiano! Eeeasy!'

That's the polite stuff. There's also the direct.

'Hey, idiot! Piss off up the road if you want to ride quicker!'

It's the same as your classic cycling club Sunday run. Always one lad who's feeling strong, finds himself next to someone a little worse for wear, and puts the squeeze on him. If you're going to join the grupetto for the day, you need to ride with their rules, at their pace. Follow the wise old owls who control the pace – someone like Bernie Eisel, a past master of this niche. Just ride as fast as they say, and you'll be grand. Let your mind wander; watch some of the fresher guests in the grupetto mess around. I remember Juan Antonio Flecha in his Rabobank days grabbing a massive American flag from a spectator who was running alongside, wearing an outsized NFL helmet complete with antlers. Flecha rode a good kilometre up the mountain before handing it back to the bloke, who appeared to be enjoying it at the time but shortly afterwards probably collapsed on the floor after realizing what sprinting up mountains at 2000m altitude does to the lungs.

If you do have excess energy, you're better off singing a song to yourself. Just understand that you won't have a choice which song it is. Your brain will hang on to the last thing you heard as you left the stage host town, some shocking piece of Euro pop coming through a PA, or something that leaked out of Wout Pouls' smartphone. You won't even know what it's about – just three words in the chorus that you've made up to fit the original Italian or Dutch. Round and round your head, falling in with your pedal stroke. Mortirolo, Mortirolo, Morti-Morti-Morti-rolo.

I've never reconned this climb. There's almost no point. You know what's coming and being punched in the face once doesn't stop it hurting the next time you're punched in the face. At least in a race you have the adrenaline to help you out a little. When that fails, you hope you have a generous team. In 2012, helping Mark Cavendish up the road, Ian Stannard grinding away beside us, we got a shout from Dave Brailsford in the second Team Sky car. 'Hang in there, guys, there's something to look forward to – we've sorted a helicopter straight from the finish to the hotel in Milan.' It's remarkable what some surprise helicopter chat can do for a broken man's morale.

There's a certain technique for riding gradients like the Mortirolo. They're too sustained to be out of the saddle trying to muscle it all the way, although you'll have to at times, even for someone like me with good seated power from a track background. You need to be more torque-y: pedalling slower with more force. Each rider has their own pedalling style, but we're all grinding. There's never really a rhythm, and so the sense of relief when the road shallows off, for even 15 metres, is immense. You're in your lowest gear and you're not coming out of it, but for a few seconds you edge up from 50rpm to 70, and it's like a cold flannel across the back of your neck. Then the steepness begins again and so does the mental battle.

And you want to ride at your own pace. Often, you'll be policing a teammate, doing a job for the team rather than purely for yourself. That's logical, and it's established practice, but it doesn't make it any easier. Riding slightly slower than you naturally want to is worse than going faster. It's less efficient. It prolongs the pain. On a faster climb you can drop your power output and feel more comfortable. Not here. You're lost in impotent rage, in your own unhappy world, in your own murky bubble of thought.

You take your relief where you can. The timing of the Giro in the calendar means it can be chilly, or at least fresh, and that works for me. The notion of riding it in the humidity of July, sweating my nuts off, is close to unpalatable. It can rain at any point round there, and that would also be taking it too far. You'd get cold, you'd feel like you were never getting out of it. And so you're grateful for the fans, the tifosi, whose support for riders of all nationalities is incredible. They get you up. If you're Italian, they get you up sometimes by pushing you quite a long way, and that's less endearing. Back in the days of the British Cycling academy, we were taught by Rod Ellingworth never to accept such an offer. Shake your head, push the helping hand away. It was seen as the same sort of crime as hanging on to a team car to get you up the field or back to a group. It's just wrong, and it's a Giro and thus a Mortirolo speciality. I've seen a Euskaltel team car come past a group of us with at least four guys all hanging on, telling us to join them.

Kiwi lead-out man Julian Dean had other ideas. First the words – 'What the fuck are you guys doing?' And then actions, grabbing one guy and pulling him off the car. The other guys hanging on immediately let go and sheepishly rode up behind. 'Sweet work, Skiddy, good on ya mate!' We might all like to do it, but it's not fair. You get pushed halfway up the Mortirolo and you're going to be a lot fresher for a final day time-trial round Milan than your rivals. Get yourself up, however slowly, or go home, because if you can't, you're not good enough to be at the finish.

By 2012, my Giro was less about survival, more about lead-outs and a big workload with the London Olympics' team pursuit coming up. Sky had Rigo Urán and Sergio Henao, both in the top ten, so my job was to help them for as long as possible. I was still a track rider, so come the Mortirolo there was a strict limit to what I could do. See you later, lads, I'm off out back to the grupetto to keep Cav and Stannard company. Bring on the sweets, the camaraderie, the bonding. While making sure we aren't chatting, of course.

Monaco

Col de la Madone

Quick note - Madone and Èze are both in France, but I ride them from Monaco so that's how I think of them. Anyway, is this the most famous climb to race up that's never been featured in an actual race?

Everyone seems to know the Madone, for good reasons and bad: because Lance Armstrong used it as his favourite training climb when he was doing a load of the bad things that led to bad scenarios; because so many of the current pros who live in the south of France use it now to do better things; because there's a best-selling bike range named after it.

I was slow in every sense when I first rode it. I hadn't heard the stories about Tony Rominger's epic training rides up it in the 1990s. I associated Lance more with Girona in Spain, because he wasn't living in Nice for long. I was aware that there was a Trek Madone, yet incapable of putting one and one together to realize where the company that supplied bikes to a man who liked riding the Col de Madone had got their inspiration from. 'Hey, what are the chances of that?'

I also went up it like a man towing a fridge. Chris Froome had been living in the area longer than me, and he threw the Madone in as a cruel digestif at the end of a brutal day's training that had also included something known locally as the Boonen Climb. All you need to know about the Boonen Climb is that it's savage and steep, and that I was still wasted from it as I followed Froome's enthusiastic waving up the Madone, which instantly finished me off.

Now? Me and the Madone are mates, sort of. And I definitely think of it as iconic, although for pretty different reasons. You could know all the usual stuff about the Madone – Lance, the bike, Richie Porte's Strava record – and you still wouldn't think about it as we do.

Partly because you wouldn't associate it with a drummer. And I do, because right at the very top, just before the last hairpin going left, there is a man who sits there on a gravelly corner with a full drum kit in front of him – bass, snare, toms, cymbal, high hat. It's as if he has been cut out of a photo of a nightclub down on the Côte d'Azur and glued on to the backdrop of pine trees and pale stone walls that you get on the top of the Madone. Except that far from being motionless, he's thrashing away like Keith Moon.

The first few times you see him, you stare. You ask the obvious questions of your training partners: did I really see that? What's he doing here? Who gave him that polka-dot King of the Mountains t-shirt? After a while, you sack off thoughts of obsessing over a quick time and actually pull over and ask him yourself.

Turns out to be entirely logical. He loves playing the drums, his wife hates him playing the drums. Rather than end his relationship over a steady four-beats-to-the-bar rhythm, he packs his kit in the boot and back seat of his Peugeot 305, drives up the steepest road he knows and sets it all up again in the arse-end of nowhere. The t-shirt came from a rider he'd inadvertently entertained for months. Same for the cycling cap he sports on sunny days.

There was a period of time when he went missing. It made the Madone a more agonizing climb than it had been since the fateful day of the Boonen/Froome double-header. Was he ill? Had his wife left him, meaning he was now hammering away in an otherwise empty house, tears rolling down his cheeks? The relief as I edged my way round the final few bends one morning to hear a thump-thump-tsst-tssst gradually getting louder was intense. When I saw him, grinning away behind his red toms and big black bass drum, I was close to tears myself. You're back! You're alive!

That's the drummer. Then there are the dogs. On the way up, less than ten minutes in, there's always a hound that comes from nowhere to throw himself at the bars of a gate to a house, and not to cheer you on like the drummer. It's a dog with serious anger-management issues: teeth out, drool out, growl on.

Cyclists don't tend to be massive fans of dogs when we're out on our bikes. They're too random, too manic.

They can aid your pursuit of a quick time if they chase you, for sure, but you can't trust them. They're like fans on Alpe d'Huez who have banged down three lagers too many – they might think they're being friendly, that running alongside you is the greatest idea ever, but they're wrong, and they're likely to get a squirt of energy drink in the chops to tell them so.

The dog on the lower slopes of the Madone is angry but he's also confused. There's a contradiction at the heart of his existence that he can't seem to resolve. If the gate's shut, he hits it with the fury and frustration of a prisoner serving a life sentence. Yet when it's open, which is quite often, he finds himself incapable of crossing the threshold, as if habit or some invisible force is holding him back. He's like Morgan Freeman's character in *The Shawshank Redemption*. He wants to be free, but he doesn't. He hates his confinement, but he finds great comfort in it, too.

You ride for another fifteen minutes, and you meet two more dogs. This time they're out on the road with a load of goats. I told you you didn't know the Madone. These dogs are huge, great white things that like chasing goats only slightly less than they like chasing cyclists. I believe the correct name for them is Pyrenean mountain dogs. They're loyal to the farmers and fiercely protective of the goats, which might explain why they chase us. People talk in awe about that time that Richie set on this climb, speculate that he had some sort of sweet tailwind. I can only assume he had a day without Bottom Dog, Goat-Dogs and the drummer.

There used to be another dog. Top Dog. Maybe the worst of all. He had the anger of Bottom Dog and the enthusiasm of Goat-Dogs. The only good thing about Top Dog was how high on the climb you'd encounter him. He was actually on the very start of the descent, so if you could carry enough speed over the top, you'd be okay. You might have to take the first slight bends quicker than you ideally would have chosen, but if it meant getting away from that thing, I was all in. And while wet days added another dimension – less speed round those bends, more danger – having mates alongside you was a huge boon. Tactics: nail your position at the front, get your head down, never look back. And never be the last man over the top. If Top Dog's half-asleep in the sun, the first man will wake him and the rest instantly become targets. Even if he goes for someone in front of you, there's always you as his back-up option; or dessert, if he gets an earlier bite in.

And so the details. It's about thirteen kilometres long, the Madone, although it depends precisely where you begin your effort. Averages around 7%, never gets above 10%. But it drags, and the gradient fluctuates, and it's hard, no matter what shape you're in.

There are different ways up it. The classic is from the

Menton side, right on the border between France and Italy. William Webb Ellis, the man who supposedly invented rugby, is buried in the town's graveyard, although this may be of more interest to Welsh cyclists than the Belgians or Spanish. Some people start at the little Intermarché super-market on the left as you leave Menton on the D22, but we tend to wait until you've done a couple of roundabouts and a brace of bends, and go when you see the bus stop on the other side of the road to the one you're climbing.

Almost straight away you see the thin concrete strip of the A8 autoroute bridge way up above you. That's the road that runs along the coast, all the way past Nice and Cannes and onwards, and confusingly, it will keep appearing on this climb – above you twice, underneath you shortly afterwards, down below in the distance by the sea as you get closer to the top.

It's all wiggles and little bends, the Madone, the road grippy and yet loose in other places, starting narrow and pinching off even more as you climb. For the first fifteen minutes or so you're protected slightly from the Mediterranean heat by the tree cover. Later, the sun will be beating down on your back, bouncing back off the stone walls and the pale road surface. You feel yourself slowly cooking, glad of your sunglasses if you have them, getting thirstier with each kilometre that you grind out.

It's a climb where you can feel great at the start, give it some beans thinking you're on a good one and then gradually get worn down by how long it is. There is never any real let-up. You've been riding hard for eighteen minutes, and you're blowing, and you look up and realize you've still got another thirteen/fifteen minutes to go.

You hang on for the little village of St Agnès, maybe twenty or so minutes in, depending how well you're going. It looks beautiful – stone houses cascading down the mountainside – and if you're on a cruisey day, you could stop for coffee here. If you're not, you take the sharp left turn and take a deep breath for another twelve/thirteen minutes of the road disappearing upwards in front of you.

There is a brief, easier section coming up. You can think of this as a good thing, but a strange phenomenon can happen up here. When you're doing a hard time-trial effort and you're tired and the gradient goes away a little, it messes with your rhythm. The gradient gives you something to push against, even if you've spent the previous 8km wishing it would push off. You lose your concentration; you lose your speed. If you're just riding up a climb, it's much nicer having it tough on the lower section and then easing off. If you're trying to nail it bottom to top, you want it consistent. When you hit the easier section and find yourself legless, it's then even more difficult getting back into your rhythm for the tough final five minutes. It's like when you're trying to push-start a mate's car. The hardest bit is getting it moving again, not keeping it rolling at the same speed.

And yet. If you're not doing that non-stop effort, the Madone drags like little else. When you're preparing for a Grand Tour, eating less, training more, you're in a perpetual state of weakness and hunger. That goes away if you're racing or buried in the pain of an effort. When you're just getting up it, it can take forty-five minutes. That's slow. That's Test match pain. It's 925 metres high at the top, and you feel yourself counting every single one of them.

The other route to the summit is longer but shallower. It makes a great time-trial effort, up from the coast, gradual all the way, not too far from home. From Menton, you head straight up the Grande Corniche to La Turbie, take a sharp hairpin right and continue to climb, followed by a long 6/7km false-flat plateau. Personally, I hate this section – maybe because I've ridden it a lot, maybe because it's where Richie and I, teammates at the time, both crashed on a rain-soaked stage of Paris-Nice when we were virtual first and second on GC. Anyway, at the end of this drag, it's another hairpin right, and you're on the backside of the Madone. Technically, only the last 20% of this route is on the actual Madone. Whatever. It's still the back way up to me.

So it's the first side that gets all the attention, and it's so close to Monaco that you will always see another pro going up it or coming down. There are more riders than cars, which is always a good thing. And while there are always guys like Luke Rowe who hate it, there are others like Richie who can't get enough of it. I'd say three-quarters of his training rides either begin or end with the Madone. He would be delighted if they did ever manage to get a proper stage race going up it, although the road's too narrow to make it work and the space at the top too limited for a finish area. Maybe you could climb it and then descend to a finish in Nice. Richie?

I've never had a blinder on it. In the first few years I would use it to throw in a few spikes in an otherwise steady climb, rather than doing the balls-out bottom to top against the clock as Lance apparently used to do. Then it became more of an over-under effort, where I went hard to St Agnès and then stayed at threshold until the top, which means holding the sort of pace I could race at for an hour, rather than my flat-out maximum.

My best is just under thirty-one minutes, which came in the build-up to the 2015 Tour as I started to find my true climbing legs for the first time. Anything quicker than that is real shifting. Richie's PB is sub-30, which reflects his taste in climbs, too. If there were a world hill-climb championships of the sort they have across Britain in September and October, he'd clean up every time. Give him a one-off climb and he's the happiest man in France.

Then again, he's never crashed coming down it, as I have. I was on my TT bike when I hit a stone, had a brief moment of truth as both my hands came off the bars, and then hit the deck hard. It was one of the worst I'd ever had, for a crash in training carries none of the protection that the adrenaline of racing brings. I sat there by the side of the road with my training partner Ben Swift, no skin left on the palms of my hands, not a great deal left on my legs. Ben had invited a mate out with us on his scooter, partly to carry some water bottles for us, mainly for the fun of it. Looking at his face as he stared at this bloke bleeding all over the pavement, I got the sense that he felt he'd been sold a dud.

And so when I think about the Madone, I think about all those things. But I also think of it like that bloke you know in your local pub who has always been there. You have a quick chat with him on your way in, but you also appreciate he's a big unit, and you don't want to get on the wrong side of him. He's a builder, got his own business, member of the darts team. He was in there when you went in with your dad for the first time for your debut pint, and whenever you pop in now when you're back home visiting, he's always there for a chat. But you never linger too long. He knows you, and you know him. Friendly, but always slightly wary, too.

Col d'Èze

15/03/2015, final stage of Paris-Nice, time-trial
Tim Kerrison: 'The final stage of the race. G had crashed
the day before. The conditions were slow, with a headwind
in the faster section of the course towards the top. Richie
Porte's winning time of 20:23 was more than a minute
slower than his winning time two years before. G finished
39 seconds behind Richie – only good enough for seventh
on the stage, and fifth on GC.'
13/03/2016, final stage of Paris-Nice, road stage
Tim Kerrison: 'G was in the yellow jersey, but Alberto
Contador was sitting second, 15 seconds down and racing
aggressively. For the same section as the TT a year earlier,
G's time was more than a minute faster.'
Duration: 19 mins 57 secs
Distance: 9.37km
Ave speed: 27.9kph
Ave power: 376w
Ave cadence: 88

On the descent, chasing Contador:
Duration: 12 mins 37 secs

Distance: 12.9km
Ave speed: 61.6kph

It's a special climb, the Col d'Èze, for the role it has traditionally played on the final day of the first proper stage race of the year, Paris-Nice. Races have been won and lost there. From the capital to the coast, racing for the sun. Big names and great days, the blue of the Mediterranean ahead of you, the villas and hills behind.

But it's special, too, for everything it's not. The Èze seems small, but it isn't. It seems easy, but it never is. It's a small, wiry man who keeps coming up to you in the pub, challenging you to an arm-wrestle: 'I'll have you, I will!' You look at him, can't see anything going on in the bicep area and think: nah, I'll have *you*. He doesn't look strong. He doesn't do big weights in the gym while looking in the mirror. He doesn't even own a mirror. He's never picked up a dumbbell and he's never done isolated curls.

He doesn't have to. He can do fifty pull-ups without appearing to try. He does the pull-ups off the branch of a tree in his local park. He does them in an old t-shirt he got for free. It's probably got Fido Dido on the front. And he'll beat you in that arm-wrestle, because you've forgotten how hard he is, and he's going to come at you from the off and before you know it you'll be blowing out of your backside and going backwards fast.

That's the Col d'Èze.

It's the climb that never feels like a climb – if you live down in Monaco or Nice, as half the world's pro road cyclists seem to, and it's part of your daily commute. It's ten kilometres long, but it only averages just under 5%. The Madone is the famous one coming out of Nice but we do Èze even more, unless you're Luke Rowe and you'd rather go the quicker, easier way along the flat coastal road, than get on the pedals for an extra fifteen minutes. It's got a spectacular view at the summit, way over to houses and beaches down below on the right, but you don't ever feel that high up. Even at the start, by Hotel Le Panoramic, it's not that panoramic. It's mainly the backside of high-rise flats. And a lot a blue sky, to be fair.

But it is a climb, and it's a climb from the start. There's no riding into it. It kicks up from the bottom, and if you're coming into it on Paris-Nice, you'll be fighting for a good position near the front. The run-in can be treacherous because the corners are tight and can be slippery. When it rains – and it can come down properly at that time in March – the road can turn into a river.

I've been caught out a few times. There was the time we could see black storm clouds off in the distance. 'Ah, we'll be fine, we'll make it up and down Èze before the storm. See you later, Luke!' Two kilometres later and the rain is hammering. Not normal rain. Not even Welsh rain. The type of rain where each raindrop seems to be the size of a ping-pong ball. We try to take cover under some trees. But in the ten minutes it takes to pass, the road has become a fast-flowing river to swim up, as well as climb.

It's steep on the Èze and solid, and you're on the defensive almost immediately. You're into it, and you're breathing hard, when you get a slight slackening off for five or ten seconds. Then it drags up again, eases off in the middle section where they have the time check in Paris-Nice if it's a time-trial, and then it kicks up again. This is how Èze behaves: up and down, messing with your head, messing around with your rhythm. Even the last kilometre, where it eases off again, it's all about the deception – because you can see a corner ahead and start thinking it's the last one, because you can't see any more. But the reason you can't see any more is that the road sneaks left behind a hill, and so it's always the corner after the next one, rather than the one you're on. Even if you know Èze intimately and have ridden it fifty times in a year, when you're racing up it on empty and you're seeing stars it always catches you out.

You have to be aggressive. You can't pace a time-trial up there. You can't build into it, or you'll have tossed away too much time by the point you start laying it all down towards the top. Go full-on from the bottom, hold that pace in the middle, hang on towards the top. It's deceitful enough that I've never had a great experience racing up it. Even when I won Paris-Nice in 2016 I was distanced at the time check and had to frantically chase down Richie Porte and Alberto Contador on the descent back towards the Promenade des Anglais. When I time-trialled it to the summit finish I tried to pace it and build my speed to the top, and I didn't give myself enough to build on.

Someone will always fall into those familiar traps. A big name will always lose time; lose a GC podium place or the lead. Paris-Nice is one of the hardest races of the year, because every day is full-on. The other stage races early in the year have their lulls. Paris-Nice? Every day seems windy. For the first seven you race hard. On the eighth you scrap your way into Nice and then meet the Èze. There's nothing nice about it.

Here's the way to play it. It's the final climb of the eight days, so you know a rider from one of the teams will seize the chance to take it on. It's a wide road, so it's easy enough to move up if you have the legs, but you don't want to expend all your energy at the bottom; there's twenty minutes of climbing to come. Wait for the set of traffic lights about 1.5 kilometres in, move up on that short descent, work your way into a good position before the second steep section.

Riders get complacent here. They think they're almost there, Paris in the distant past, the finish line and a drink and a massage within touching distance. The road is smooth and the route profile that you looked at in the morning on the team bus says it flattens out any moment. This is where you want to go, when guards have been lowered and everyone is on their limits, just as the steep part comes to an end and everyone is looking at everyone else. If there's a headwind, hold back a little longer, suck a few wheels and then launch. You don't want to drag people with you. If it's still, throw in the big attack. When the road starts twisting and hugging the grooves and troughs of the mountain, you can be out of sight within twenty seconds, and even if your lead is a slim one, it can appear far more substantial.

If you're a pure climber, you want a variation on that. Get your team to ride a solid pace at the front through the middle flatter section, so none of your rivals can use that interlude to recover from the first kick. Then, as you hit that second steep section, accelerate away and get your gap. The issue you might have is that the road is pretty straight here. For about 500 metres, you'll be in view, all the way to a slight left, and even then, you're never gone. And while you're in view, you're in danger. You're the hare and they're the hounds.

Here's your next problem, whichever way you play it: if it's not a summit finish, if you are heading back into the city – well, it's hard to hang on to that advantage on the descent. You need a good twenty seconds in your pocket to have any chance of holding on. If there's two or more of you – better chance. You could have ten seconds, but if you work together, taking turns, switching smoothly, and if the chase pack look at each other and try to get someone else to stick their nose in the wind and lead the pursuit – now you could stay away.

There are climbs in this book where I'll recommend you change your gearing to help you through them. Almost invariably this will be a bigger sprocket on the back, or smaller chainring on the front, the winch to drag you up something where ordinary gearing would leave you stalling. Èze is the only one where you want a bigger chainring on the front, and it's all because of that descent. The night before the deciding day in Paris-Nice in 2016, me in the leader's jersey by fifteen seconds from Contador after the mountainous penultimate stage, I lay in bed all evening trying to imagine how various scenarios might play out the next day. Fifteen seconds on Contador, a great climber, and only six more on Richie, who knew these hills around Nice as well as anyone. At 11 o'clock at night I texted Sky's sporting director, Nico Portal. 'Nico, can you get them to stick a 54 on the bike for tomorrow?'

Fifty-four teeth on my big chainring – more to push against, more to power me down a descent. And I needed it, because Contador and Richie had thirty seconds on me going over the top, and I had to chase like a lunatic with Sergio Henao and Tony Gallopin on the 15km descent and flat section to the finish on the Promenade des Anglais. And we made it, near enough – thirty seconds sliced and chopped back to just five seconds, which meant that with the time bonus Contador got for second place,

I won an eight-day race by four seconds. All thanks to the chainring, plus Sergio, and not forgetting Tony, who I promised afterwards I'd buy a beer the next time the two of us were watching Wales beat France in the Six Nations.

So those are the racing memories. Most of the time it's training, and it's slightly more sedate, and you can smell the pine trees and feel the warmth coming back off the pale road and white-painted houses when spring starts creeping in and the grey of winter slinks away. Especially towards the top, it's genuinely pretty. You can glance down at the coastline, at the sea, at the woods on the promontory of Cap Ferrat, and think, which of these multi-million-pound houses would I live in if I had the choice?

You know Elton John lives over there. You're aware that Bono has got one of the big ones in Èze itself. You can look down at the yachts in the harbour and work out which are really big by the fact that they have smaller boats piggybacked on top of them for the short run to shore. You can take a photo of the huge cruise liners that stop off in port and text it to your mother-in-law and tell her it's actually the private super-cruiser of Roman Abramovich, and have a little chuckle when she replies, 'Wow! Amazing! But that's too big, the silly man.'

There's even a house there that Mark Cavendish claims is the most expensive house in the entire world. It's a very Cav thing, to be as definitive as that about something that he's by no means an expert on, but maybe he's right on this occasion. It's huge. A small road runs through the outer gardens, and there's a bridge to take you over it. The gates at the front are as wide as the street I grew up on in Cardiff. The view is laughably good. It's on the podium, even if it's not the overall winner.

One final favourable thing about Èze. The cars on it tend to behave. Drivers know cyclists train on it and so they either behave or they do a Luke and choose to stick to the coastal road instead. All except one old boy I saw once, careering down towards the flatter time-trial check section on a day when the rains had come and the road surface had all the grip of a wok. As I came round one corner, he came round the one in front sliding sideways. As I slammed on my brakes, he touched his and accelerated his pirouette, smashing into a wall before coming to a halt with his engine still running, facing back the way he had come.

I would have been out of the car and calling for an ambulance. This guy just drove back up the hill, as if nothing had happened, as if he had just stopped at an old mate's house for a coffee and croissant. Just styling it out.

Very Nice. Very Èze.

USA

Saddle Peak: Las Flores

22/01/2020, training ride, doing a spiked, submaximal effort, so not full gas but not hanging around, either
Duration: 29 mins 09 secs
Distance: 9.28km
Ave speed: 18.8kph
Ave power: 398w
Ave cadence: 76

This may come as a surprise to you, but Americans are actually pretty good at pronouncing the name Geraint. None of the rushing it you get in some places, the G'runts, or the leaving out of key vowels to give you Ger-rant. The only problem I've had in Los Angeles, riding through the Santa Monica mountains, was from a bloke in a car who saw my branded jersey, my Pinarello, and thought: full-kit wanker.

'Hey man! Who do you think you are, Geraint Thomas?'

I glanced across at him. 'Morning!'

He was three seconds into a full-on belly laugh when a switch flicked in his brain.

'Holy shit, you *are* Geraint Thomas!'

And so I've felt at home in California, ever since I

started heading there for warm-weather training at the start of each season. I'd estimate less than 50% of the people I meet there know where Wales is. I'm not sure that many know *what* Wales is. But my cultural outreach programme is touching more people each year, and I've had my own education to complete, too. My assumption was that Los Angeles was all about the car and the freeway. I knew about Rodeo Drive and the Hollywood sign. I didn't think about bikes, and I didn't think about steep empty roads. And then I spoke to Cam Wurf, road racer turned Ironman triathlete turned back to rider, who has ridden out here for years, and is also coached by Tim Kerrison. And I dipped a toe in one January, and there was bike love everywhere you looked: great cafés, lovely little bike shops, early-morning group rides all over the place. Tim went out on one organized by someone at 21st Century Fox through our Sky connection, expecting a gentle pedal with some portly movie types. Two hours later he was in small Aussie pieces, blown apart by relentless chain-gang-style efforts along the Pacific Coast Highway and up the Las Flores climb.

And so now the year starts with an LA story. My wife Sa and I will get a little place on Airbnb in Pacific Palisades, the next town along from Santa Monica. I'll ride each morning while she and our son Macs can take a stroll or go to the beach. She will probably have the more relaxing time.

Because of the four ways you can get to the top of Saddle Peak, Las Flores is the hardest. Straight up the canyon road from the Pacific Coast Highway, a drag of 500 metres or so at the start, then a kick up and a continuation. You go past a little park on your left and then see the tarmac rising in front of you at 15%. Quick tip: if you're struggling, there's a petrol station – okay, gas station – at the bottom where you can pick up a vast bottle of American pop that comes with enough caffeine and E numbers that you'll still be buzzing when you're in bed.

On the Col d'Èze, in Nice, you know you're going uphill but you don't feel it – not unless you're racing. You definitely feel Las Flores. There's an option after a kilometre or so, just after a hairpin to the left, where you can opt for an easier route to the top – draggy, for sure, but never brutal. Cam likes to go that way. Not all Ironmen are men of iron. If you stay on the canyon road, the buildings to either side drop away, and there are no more of the white signs that read 'SPEED LIMIT 25', which doesn't matter to us anyway on a road this steep. Like Èze, too, there are supposedly many celebrity homes around the area, Pamela Anderson reportedly being one of them, although I've never seen her. I don't know why I'd expect to; I'm pretty sure she doesn't ride a bike, and she'd probably have a nice air-conditioned gym along with personal trainer for any exercise she chooses to do.

Anyway. Now the road starts to slice through the scrub and the red soil, the canyon cutting straight up the hillside. You can't see the top, but you can see a long way up, and it's probably best not to think about that too much. Don't let the mile markers get you down, either. When you're used to kilometres on the Continent, you can initially get a little boost from the switch away from metric. There seems to be less of whatever's being counted left. What, only four more until the top? Get in! But a mile crawls where a kilometre skims by, and it's a hollow victory. Kilometres stack up, but they don't hang around.

They're so pale, American roads, the white lines on the outside and the thick yellow one down the middle. You can see black tyre marks on the steeper sections as cars have revved their way up, and on the outside of the tighter bends when they squealed on the way down. The rocks come in steep and tight off to your left and the mountain slips away to your right as you climb, and the sun starts to get you here: pleasantly so in January, when there's often a cheeky ocean breeze to dry your sweat too; cruelly so, if you're having a pop in July or August. Only on the lower slopes do you start getting a little shade, the pines leaning over the road, the smell of their needles in your nostrils.

The earlier sections – they have me thinking of Yosemite. Which I appreciate is a long way off, but it's the colour of the rocks, the steep embankments. As you climb, it becomes more reminiscent of scenes from *Breaking Bad* or *Narcos* – that southern Californian and New Mexico scrub, the stunted bushes, the bright blue skies. This is where the unwary start to feel it in their legs. Riding it with Cam and my teammate Ben Swift, I'll generally pull away a little around this point, hear them speed up in pursuit, listen to them starting to mutter and then look over my shoulder a few bends on to see nothing but empty road. At the top of the climb I'll hear the excuses that were cooked up on the remainder of the session: 'oh, we thought it was a sixteen-minute effort only; oh, I did this twice yesterday.' It's a climb where once you're gone, you're gone. And while I personally have no beef with the descending abilities of Ironmen and triathletes, it's a road so steep that Cam prefers to ride up it rather than down. There's no snappy comebacks here.

There's a brashness about it, Las Flores. It could only really be in the US. It's loud but it's friendly. There's loads going on – corners, turn-offs, scenery – and it's not shy about it. You'd happily introduce him to your mates, and they'd love his company on a night out. The hangover would be intense, but no one would forget it. And you'd go back for more, because he's noisy but he's fun, and he's endearing, in his own ostentatious way.

When you exit the trees there's a little respite from the gradient as the sunshine comes into play. You turn right on to a bigger road, and although you're now battling 7% rather than 10% it's still hard going. Another pleasant aspect of my LA education was discovering that the drivers you encounter here will give you space and respect. There'll be the odd hooligan banging on his horn, but most hang back until there's space to overtake – even the big wagons hauling themselves up. I had one who was polite enough to wait behind for me to get round a corner, only to lose all momentum and stall. I could hear his engine roaring impotently as I pulled away, a slight sense of guilt in my slipstream.

Your fellow riders are on point with protocol, too. The doomsday scenario when riding overseas is the ghost teammate – the one who spots you on a day when you're going long, eating little and going slow, buries themselves to catch up and then sits silently on your wheel for the next ten minutes, taking surreptitious videos and uploading them to Facebook. 'Yeah, just been riding with Geraint Thomas, found the pace a bit easy to be fair; he tried to drop me but didn't have the legs.' The LA gang are instead respectful in a cool way: ten seconds of chat, a smile, and off. 'Hey, man, how's it going? Yeah? Yeah? Okay, man, have a great day! Laters!'

There's also an old boy who runs around these hills barefoot. Each year I see him out here at least three times a week, and that's just when we bump into him. He always has on the same wide-brimmed hat, just knocking out the miles. Intrigued, I stopped last year and asked why. His reply? He was training for the London Marathon. Turns out he's eighty years old and has the world record for his age group. He told me he moved to the US thirty-odd years ago and considers it the greatest country in the world because anyone can go there, work their arse off and be successful. It's a good moral to have in your mind as you're slogging up Las Flores: this is good for me. It might all pay off.

Okay. We're almost there. Seven hundred metres more on the main road, a right turn and then the final mile to the summit. You can see Saddle Peak ahead of you, look back at the Pacific and Malibu nestled up next to it. As you push for the top, you find yourself almost confused. How can I be in the wilderness when half an hour ago I was in Santa Monica?

It's calm, up there. Calm like the top of the Èze, maybe calmer still than the Col de la Madone, because there's no lone drummer and no succession of rogue dogs. And you need to get your breath back, because it's the toughest ascent you'll find in those mountains, and in early January you're still carrying the sins and good times of Christmas around your middle. The first time up Las Flores in the first week is punishing. Two weeks on and its repeated privations have skimmed off some of the excess weight and put a punch in your legs that wasn't there before. You can feel the speed returning and you're glad, despite how much it hurts getting to that point, and you appreciate the warmth and the lack of rain and the views that just take the slightest edge off the punishment. Also that it's not July; Cam has told me stories of being so hot and going so slow that when sweat has dripped off him he's seen it hit the ground and dry before he's even ridden past.

There's another similarity with Èze. Just as there are heaps of little roads that can get you from the corniche in Nice to the empty inlands, so you have loads of options heading north out of LA off the Pacific Coast Highway, almost all of them through quiet residential neighbourhoods, challenging at the bottom and view-filled at the top. It's why you bump into other pro riders – Cannondale or Axel Merckx's team – hanging round Pedalers Fork café and bike shop in Calabasas, sampling their own blend of beans, sitting out in the sun before a gentle stretch out on the way home.

In Pacific Palisades, Sa and I can go out for an evening stroll, try a new restaurant, be flummoxed once again by the tipping system. Have I left enough? The waitress is smiling, but they're always smiling in LA. You could dump your food on the floor and they'd still smile at you. They take your drink away, fill it up and bring it back. Great, but are we paying for this? Right, they've done it again, I hope so, otherwise we've just done $80 on soft drinks.

But LA is set up for road riders in ways it doesn't even realize. In most places in the States the portions are way too big for us skinny boys. You can't get a scoop of ice cream, you have to get a bucket. Everything comes with extra fries. Everything comes with cheese. 'Maple syrup on your sweet potatoes, sir?' 'Sorry, what?' In LA, they're even more obsessive than us. Vegan. Gluten intolerant. Paleo. Every meal is free of something.

I'm looking forward to going back when I'm retired. Two weeks of pigging out, of having at least two unnecessary extra things added to every dish. Syrup potatoes for breakfast, overly large meat for tea. I'll put two stone on in two weeks and never go up Las Flores once. Unless it's in a car.

France

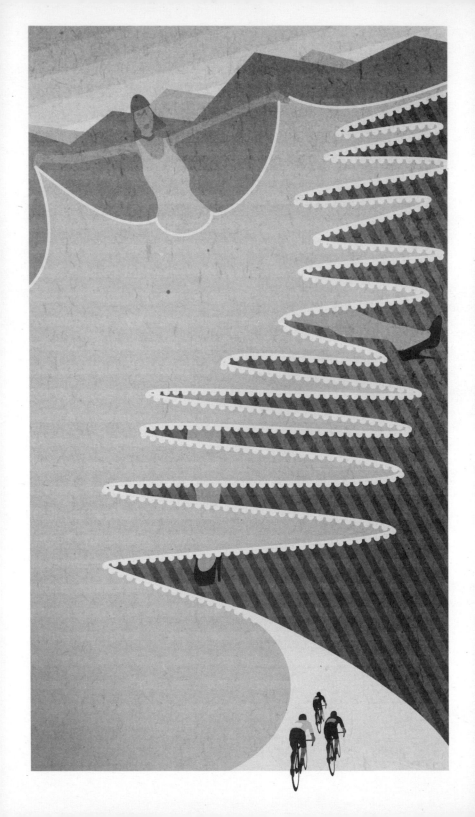

Planche des Belles Filles

5/7/2017, Tour de France
Tim Kerrison: 'G was in the yellow jersey, but lost 40 seconds to Fabio Aru on the stage, and lost the yellow jersey to Chris Froome.'
Duration: 12 mins 25 secs
Distance: 3.95km
Ave speed: 18.5kph
Ave power: 402w
Final kick, from last hairpin after car park:
Duration: 59 secs
Distance: 0.28km
Gradient: 13.8%
Ave speed: 16.7kph
Ave power: 495w

10/7/2019, Tour de France stage six
Final kick, from last hairpin after car park, this time with additional 1.25km ramp to follow:
Duration: 50 secs
Distance: 0.25km
Gradient: 12.4%
Ave speed: 18.4kph
Ave power: 548w

Final 1.25km – on to gravel, then steep ramp to finish:
Duration: 3 mins 26 secs
Distance: 1.25km
Ave speed: 21.3kph
Ave power: 486w
Ave cadence: 87
VAM (vertical altitude metres, aka your vertical speed in metres per hour): penultimate section, 2214; final ramp, 1942
Tim Kerrison: 'For comparison, on the Tour climb from Mende in 2018, G had a VAM of 1988, which is really high, probably his highest over a medium length climb.'

You hear a lot about the Alps and the Pyrenees. Not least from me, in this book. I'm not blaming anyone; they're spectacular places to ride uphill on your bike. But let's not forget the Vosges in all this, even if many outside France would struggle to locate them on a map.

They're strange, the Vosges mountains. Dark and green like the Pyrenees. Forested and damp, where the Alps in summer are clean and bright. They're shallower by the standards of the two big brothers, and there are no spectacular snow-capped peaks. There are no hour-long climbs.

That's fine. They're special in their own slightly suspicious way; they're hidden and they're quirky and they're not entirely trusting of strangers. They almost feel like an outpost of the Basque country, transported hundreds of miles north-east towards the border with Germany rather than Spain. And I like them, with their twisty, narrow roads, the little picturesque towns, the passion of their cycling fans. You come to the Vosges on your way to somewhere else in the Tour de France, but they're never just a stopover. They're a set piece and a fierce challenge all on their own.

Planche des Belles Filles doesn't make sense, as a climb or a place. Some people will tell you it gets its name from a massacre in the Thirty Years' War, when a group of women – the beautiful girls of the 'belles filles' – threw themselves in a lake to avoid their pursuers. Others go for the more prosaic theory that it's about the beech trees on the mountain, called 'fahys' in the old Jura dialect, and that 'belles fahyes' has gradually been corrupted. Either way, it's almost as hard to pronounce properly as it is to ride up. Native English speakers tend to start off well but get over-confident after nailing Planche des, stumble over Belles and then collapse on Filles. It's the same when you're climbing it. The bottom is okay and lures you in. The middle is uncomfortable. The finale is a brutal mess, a ramp that feels like going up a ski jump the wrong way and then a gravel track that should really be ridden on a cyclo-cross bike. It only adds to its allure. There's nowhere else quite like it.

My own experiences are mixed. The first time I rode it, in the 2017 Tour, I began the climb in the yellow jersey and ended it as Chris Froome's premier domestique. I'd had a bad crash at the Giro two months before and wasn't climbing at my best, and there's no hiding on that road. Just under 6km that day (the race organizers had yet to hatch their evil gravel extension plan), an average gradient of slightly less than 9%. And you find that you can be on your absolute limit but just about surviving, getting over a steep ramp, taking a slight breather, wondering if you might be able to hang on despite having no rhythm at all, because the gradient keeps going steep-shallow-steep-shallow, and you can see the finish arch 300 metres ahead – and suddenly, the road goes stupid and lifts off at 24%. That's not a road, it's the side of a house. And if you're feeling in any way sub-par at that point, you're gone straight away. You can cycle 250m on the flat in the time it takes to type this sentence. When you're climbing Planche des Belle Filles, you can lose half a minute on it. Warning: steepness kills.

It's not actually as long or high as the Ballon d'Alsace. But because the Ballon is usually served as an hors d'oeuvres on a Tour stage and Planche as the entrée, it's the latter that draws your fire. It's almost like a mini Zoncolan, but whereas that Italian climb is known as the Monster and is attractive to no one, Planche seems significantly more achievable. Of course it's steep. But it's a road that gives you a lot back. It's not straight up a bleak hillside. It has twists, trees, goes hard and then backs off. You can enjoy it – in the way you can enjoy a craft beer that's 11% and doing you significant damage with every sip. If you're reconning it, you can even take a little breather on the slight downhill section before the Wall of Death.

It's dark, at the bottom, in among the trees. Almost spooky. You can imagine witches in the Vosges. You can imagine elves and possibly dragons. The fans are packed in at the top, so this part is quiet, maybe rain dripping off the trees, and you can lose track of what's going on. In 2017, Fabio Aru attacked early, and I thought, okay, let him go, we'll bring him back gradually as he tires. And then I switched off for thirty seconds, and he'd snatched a load of time from us. On Planche, it's hard to bring all that back. There's always a chance, but there's not much road to do the catching, and if someone is travelling as well as Aru, there's never a real let-up. It might slacken from 15% to 8%, but 8% is still 4% more than the Poggio, and time and places can slip through your fingers in a couple of corners.

It's why positioning is critical. If you hit the crucial steep section and you're stuck behind a rider who's gone legless, you're going so slowly that it can be hard to get around them. Fans to one side, another rider the other side. You can't get the kick of acceleration. You lift your face from your handlebar stem and it's your front wheel, their back wheel and the cold metal of the barriers. The struggling rider takes you backwards with them.

That was me in 2014 – my first experience of riding

Planche. I'd seen the videos and heard the tales. Back then, I could hold my own on the climbs but also had to know my limits. I was riding for Richie Porte after Chris Froome had crashed out of the Tour on the cobbled stage earlier on, feeling good and hanging in the front group of twenty or so riders, the late Michele Scarponi riding on the front for his Astana team leader Vincenzo Nibali. And then we went into a corner which tightened up on the exit, touched wheels and were both down. We got back just in time for the start of the climb, but the adrenaline boost wasn't enough to outweigh the chase back to the front. I made it a couple of kilometres up the climb, lobbed a last bit of encouragement at Richie and was spat out the back once more. Which felt easier for fifteen seconds, until I realized I was still empty and still had to get up the final brutal ramp. Oh happy days.

It's where Planche is scheduled in the Tour that matters, too. In 2019, it was on stage six, the first proper mountain test of the race, and it came on a day stacked with similar but shorter climbs. And while it was never going to be as decisive as a full-on mountain day because of its comparative length, you still ended up with similar time gaps to the ones in the lead group on Alpe d'Huez in 2018. Planche matters, and the new gravel section we had that time only added to the prestige of it. It's compact under your wheels rather than loose, but it's still deep in patches, and you can still lose your wheel and momentum.

And it looks beautifully surreal, that final stretch. It looks like slow-motion cycling. Every one of us is at our maximum but we're all only doing 10kph. You don't see that in elite racing, not at the Tour when everyone's been training all year to be in peak shape. It's so steep you want to stop pedalling. It's so steep that as soon as you cross the line, you will. Within one rotation of your wheels you've come to a halt; there's no coasting for ten metres on that steepness and that gravel. Other climbs can be hard and raced to the line, but you at least limp on for a few more pedal strokes. But here, because you can't, you almost fall off your bike. You go from 100% effort and your legs full of lactate to nothing and feeling like you want to curl up in bed with an oxygen tank for an hour or so.

It's the weirdest feeling, being motionless in one spot, but with your heart rate at its maximum. The heat hits you then, even on a damp day. Your breathing sounds like a saw in your ears. Even moving at 5kph would help get some air into your lungs. Instead you try to get some water down you, and thirty seconds later you have a TV microphone under your nose, at a point you can barely remember your name, let alone reel off a detailed rundown of the climb.

I'm aware I'm selling its charms well, so if you do fancy a pop, here's a few tips. Stick a granny gear on the back. This is not the time for empty gestures of heroism. Don't attack the steep parts too hard early on; use the hairpins, ride the shallow way round the outside if there are no cars coming past. Break the climb up into sections and use the easier parts for recovery – don't stop pedalling, but get your mojo back for the steep stuff up ahead. Before the long hairpin to the right, close to the summit, take a good drink for the final push that lies ahead. No point in saving anything back now; a 20% gradient is never going to be pleasant, but particularly after twenty minutes of stiff climbing.

Think about how you're going to climb. If you're out of the saddle too much, your arms will fatigue. If you're too deep in the saddle on the super-steep bits, your weight will be too far back and you can end up on your arse after an inadvertent wheelie. Trying to make it up the gravel section? Get out of the saddle there and too far forward and you won't have enough weight over the back wheel, and you'll wheel-spin and stop. I did say it was hard.

The sort-of solution? Stay in the saddle, but sit right on the nose (which is my natural position). It'll freak you out, breathing as deeply as if you're sprinting while barely pedalling and moving so slowly, but it's the only way. Go low cadence and high power. You might feel as if you're going nowhere for an enormous effort; remind yourself what it's like doing certain sessions on your turbo-trainer at home. But you'll be sucking the air in, inviting it into every orifice, and there is no perfect position, not really – never one that can actually be described as comfortable – because this is Planche des Belles Filles, and that's the whole point.

I'm making this sound horrific, and it is when you're racing to the line. Yet in all honesty, the first five kilometres aren't any tougher than a lot of other climbs in this book. It's that final 300m, or the top of the gravel section if you're feeling fruity, that does you. You begin the stage tired. You ride for three hours and feel even worse. You ride up the Planche at threshold for twenty minutes, and then you hit the point that matters. Even 100m when you're totally empty is enough to make you contemplate instant retirement.

It can feel like a stunt, sometimes, when race organizers throw in ludicrous climbs. And Planche is ridiculously steep. But it's not ridiculously steep for a ridiculously long time. It's not hard for the sake of being hard. It's hard because it is hard.

It's also a great place to watch bike racing. You're going slower so the fans feel closer to you. They seem louder. It's more colourful. It's definitely more intimate than the Alps, which could sometimes be in Germany they're so functional: up, more up, wide roads, sensible roads. The Vosges, like the Pyrenees, are more flamboyant, but they are even more local. Tourists don't come here. They press on to Alpe d'Huez or the Tourmalet. The Alps and the Pyrenees, they're international. This feels like the most

French climb in the world. Thibaut Pinot's from ten miles away. Julian Alaphilippe – well, everyone in every corner of France loves Julian Alaphilippe.

So I think of Planche des Belles Filles as a small, aggressive Frenchman with Basque heritage. He can be chirpy; he's friendly and he's solid. He can be full of the joys of what he's doing. But he's a little pitbull, too – someone you'd want on your side if an atmosphere turned. You don't mess with him. You stand out of his eyeline, and let others wind him up instead.

And you don't forget him. Every time the Tour has come to Planche, we have left with a fresh image seared into our brains. In 2012, it was a skinny Sky rider called Froome, pulling away from everyone else, elbows sticking out, arms so thin that the three stripes down the sleeve of his Adidas jersey were wider than the limbs beneath. In 2014, it was Vincenzo Nibali taking control of a race he would never let go; in 2017, Aru, all passion and gaping mouth and joy. In 2019, it was Giulio Ciccone getting into a break that stayed away, going into yellow and celebrating with perfect Italian delight.

That's what Planche does. Delivers drama, delivers memories. And a lesson, too, for race organizers: a climb doesn't have to be super long to be unforgettable. An awful lot can go right and wrong in 6km, in the Vosges.

Col du Portet

25/7/2018, Tour de France stage seventeen
Whole climb duration: 50 mins 12 secs
Distance: 15.8km
Ave speed: 18.8kph
Ave power: 382w

First 3.5km, when pace high due to attack from Primož
Roglič:
Duration: 11 mins 38 secs
Distance: 3.51km
Ave speed: 17.9kph
Ave power: 412w
Ave heart rate: 152bpm

Last 3.5km, pace a little stop-start, HR higher, despite
lower power, illustrating effect of altitude
Duration: 10 mins 17 secs
Distance: 3.5km
Ave speed: 20.3kph
Ave power: 393w
Ave heart rate: 160bpm

Last 2km, sustained and solid, Roglič riding on the front to put time into Chris Froome; I attacked in the final 500m
Duration: 5 mins 50 secs
Distance: 1.98km
Ave speed: 20.1kph
Ave power: 425w
Ave heart rate: 163bpm

Not that famous, the Col du Portet. If you asked most people to locate it precisely on a map, they'd struggle. Alps? Pyrenees? Definitely France? No one's even quite sure what to call it. Is it the Col du or the Col de? Portay or Pour Tett?

So let's make something about it quite clear. It was the hardest single climb of all in the 2018 Tour de France. It's the hardest single climb I've done in any Tour de France since my debut back in 2007. And I really couldn't climb in 2007.

Alpe d'Huez? It's famous for all the right reasons. Mont Ventoux is famous for scary reasons. You might see both on a tea towel in the kitchen of a cycling friend. The twenty-one hairpins of the Alpe, the white and red telecoms tower at the summit of Ventoux. Portet is too long for a tea towel. People get tattoos of the Alpe hairpins on their ankles. I've even been asked to sign my autograph on one fan's Alpe tat; he then went away and got it inked in properly, which is commitment. Try the same with the

Portet and you'd have one long line of ink snaking from your ankle to your shoulder.

So little of it makes sense. Where it's tucked away, where it goes to (nowhere), the fact the top section was still all gravel and potholes and cowpats until right up close to that Tour stage in 2018.

It may only take fifteen minutes longer to race up than Alpe d'Huez. But there are the fans and hairpins around that big boy, and the parties and the noise. The Portet doesn't bother to disguise itself. Right from the start, the horrors that are coming (and not quick enough, either) are laid out right in front of you. It slaps itself down on the counter, stares into your eyes and shrugs. This is what you've bought. Get on with it. Now.

You get to the Pyrenees – because that's where you are – and the climbs are generally steeper, shorter and on a rougher surface than those you find in the Alps. The only properly long one is the Tourmalet. Down here in the south-west, soaked by Atlantic fronts, steamed in summer, you get forest and twists and turns.

The Portet feels as if it's in the wrong place. Sixteen kilometres long. An average gradient of well over 8%, almost 10km above 10%. Wide open and exposed, almost all the way. It takes you from the valley floor in the little town of Saint-Lary-Soulon all the way up to 2215 metres – 333m higher than Ventoux.

An Alpine climb in the Pyrenees; a Swiss-style,

high-mountain, high-altitude finish in Basque country. And a profile that really suits Colombians, with that steepness, that length, the altitude. It's madness, any way you look at it.

On most mornings at the Tour de France, the team principal Dave Brailsford and some of the other backroom staff will hop on their bikes and head out for a ride of their own. It can slightly mess with the minds of the fans who often congregate outside the team hotel or who see them pedalling along the stage route as the workers put barriers up along the roadside or inflate the sponsors' arches and giant emblems: did I just see four new Ineos signings, three of them carrying significant timber?

When we're in the mountains, Dave will stay in character and take on some of the climbs his riders will race up later that same day. It keeps him fit; it stimulates his mind. Did he ride the Portet? No. Would he want to ride the Portet the next time the Tour takes us up it? The thing about the Portet is that you'd be pulling your bib-shorts on, full of the joys of a summer morning, getting your jersey off the back of the chair, and then you'd glance out of the hotel window and see it looming over you, and you'd get a sudden sideways lurch in the guts. Do I really fancy that?

You might suggest to Dave that he only does the first half, which is long enough and brutal enough to leave you in bits for the rest of the day on its own, but he's ultra-competitive, like all the staff, and he'd see that as failure rather than pragmatism, and half-measures are frowned upon by people like Dave Brailsford. But if you asked me for three words that summarized my own experiences on the Portet, I'd start with relentless. I'd throw in hard. And I'd finish with savage. You don't do the Portet for fun. You have to get mentally ready for it, and you need time on your hands, because it's a black hole of energy and resolve. Let us ride it for you, Dave. That's what you pay us for.

There's no gentle easing in with the Portet. There's no warm handshake or polite exchange of pleasantries. It just grabs you by the throat and starts throwing haymakers: 10% gradient over the first kilometre; 10% in the second. Then it eases off dramatically, plummeting to a mere 9.8%. Cheers.

You hug the cliff face on your right and look left to a huge drop-off falling away back into the valley and the neat houses around the river in the town below. And it stays like that for a lifetime, pedal stroke after heavy pedal stroke, straight up into the clouds. Most climbs are sneaky swines. They hide what's coming up, tuck it behind corners or in forests. Not the Portet. From the valley floor you can see it all laid out in front of you. Right, riders, have this.

I respect that. If you're riding well out front you can look back and see your rivals strung out behind you, like pearls falling off a broken necklace, and all feels good in the world. If you're struggling and you look forward to see riders going away from you like they've got a tailwind and your nose is digging into a gale, it's hard not to feel mentally destroyed. No one puts their arm round you on the Portet. It's just cold, hard facts. You're on form. You're having a nightmare. Deal with it.

Remember the class bully at school? The Portet is the lad who waits for you at the school gates in the morning and gives you a hard time all day. There's a brief respite when you go to your maths lesson, because you're in top set and he's in the bottom, but apart from that he's relentless. That's the Portet. The unpleasantness begins and you think, how is this ever going to end?

But then it's two climbs in one. You get that first one done, the eight kilometres straight up at that unrelenting angle. Then the corners and altitude kick in, and the second half reveals its cruel face. You see these crazy switchbacks up above you, as if they began building the road and then realized the futility of trying to make it up that sort of slope and started weaving around in a panic instead. There are no trees. There's barely a bush. Bleak rock and bleached grass. The occasional cow or sheep, baffled that after hundreds of years humans have come up here on wheels.

We reconned it, the early summer before the Tour reached it in late July. It was harder winching up it then than during the race, for this is the sort of climb that calls for the thrill and fear of competition to get up it. Chris Froome was feeling under the weather, which made it doubly punishing; you want to be very much on top of the weather for a Portet, and so he had to watch Wout Pouls and me riding away, him creeping up, five kilometres further down the mountain, never giving in, suffering all the more. It was like something you would do to punish someone; the sort of penance the tough manager of an under-twenty-three team might inflict on one of his charges who had been caught misbehaving at a training camp. I was grateful that it was 2018, when I'd learned to climb and understood where my weight had to be in the mountains. Pre-2015, I would have been another 5km behind Froomey. In 2007, I would have been weeping silently and wishing I'd never left the comfort of a velodrome.

That top section was still under construction that day. The gravel was loose and the workers in high-vis were insistent that it was not possible to ride any further. We tried to look baffled, swerved round them and kept going, throwing apologetic smiles back over our shoulders. 'You'll see our mate in about fifteen minutes, give him a push if you don't mind.' We swung round the switchbacks, felt our wheels bite in the loose stone and slip a little when we tried to push harder, and began to feel the altitude hit. I kept thinking about the short tunnel that was supposed to lie ahead, a kilometre or so from the top. Get there and we were almost home. Get out of the sun, back into the saddle, push it one more time.

It's bleak up there. Not quite Ventoux bleak, but almost worse, because Ventoux is such a freak, all on its own in the middle of Provence, that white rock like nowhere else you'll race. The top of the Portet doesn't have that grandeur. It's just pale grass and wind and sky. On the Vilaflor climb on Mount Teide on Tenerife you can forget you're at 2100 metres because you're in the trees. Atop the Portet there's nothing. It's like riding up to the moon.

The altitude. That's someone sitting on your chest. You can't take in the oxygen your muscles are screaming for. It's as if you're breathing through a toilet roll tube at the bottom of the climb and a straw at the top. It's like reverse childbirth: the longer you push, the smaller the diameter gets. That's why you end up riding with your mouth hanging open, like a whale sucking in krill.

All there is to partially balance that up is the drop in temperature. In the early kilometres of the Portet in summer it's so warm your jersey is fully unzipped. You're pouring water over your head and your ears are throbbing. By the top, it's so cold your fingers are numb and your ears feel pinched. Fortunately, this works for me. I'm built less for temperatures associated with Montego Bay and more for Cardiff Bay.

There are never many fans to cheer you on through those lonely last few stretches. They don't tend to make the second half of the climb. It's too far. It's too hard, except for the one in the free Ag2R t-shirt who tried to grab me during the final 150m in 2018, only to find the power of my mighty bicep too much to hold on to. Alpe d'Huez has big verges around the hairpins where you can park up and pitch tents. The Portet clings to the side of a cliff.

And so on this climb, perhaps more than any other in the book, you have to pace it all. Don't go into the red at the bottom. Ride a steady tempo. If you're feeling good at the very end, then push on, but keep your head. It's steep at the finish. Go too early and you risk blowing up and losing minutes. Go late and you can quickly amass a much greater advantage than you might imagine. If those last 400m can take a minute and a half to ride, you can snatch fifteen seconds off a rival when they'd already assumed they were safe.

So it proved in 2018. It was a strange day, stage seventeen, that madcap 65km dash from Bagnères-de-Luchon, the gridded cyclo-cross style start that was the most half-arsed thing we did all summer. Nico Roche sent me a little voice note that morning. 'G, it'll be horrible, hold something in reserve for the second half. Don't worry about the gravel, it's nothing you can't handle.'

That was the day when Froomey was struggling again, when he wanted us to speed up when it appeared Tom Dumoulin was being dropped. But you don't gamble on the Portet. The altitude magnifies any little effort you throw in. If you're already tired, the lack of oxygen will mean it'll hurt you even more. And so, cruel though it sounds, Froomey admitting on team radio that he wasn't feeling strong gave me a huge boost. If one of the best Grand Tour riders of all time is in trouble and you're feeling okay, how could it not?

On paper, it's a climb for the pure climbers. Nairo Quintana and Dan Martin were given leeway to go off the front; neither was a danger in the general classification. But by the second half of the third week, the accumulated fatigue in your legs changes the rules. Whoever is the strongest rider at that point will have the advantage on the hardest climbs. I closed on those two in the final kilometres and I quietly fancied I could have caught them and won the stage had I needed to.

The work was done. That night Froomey took me aside in the food truck, offered his congratulations and told me he would work for me from that point. I sensed, too, that the others – Dumoulin, Primož Roglič – had now also given up on the win, and were fighting for podium places instead.

Maybe you'll set yourself your own challenge. Try to knock off all the climbs in this book. If you do – and I like the idea – the Portet will be the hardest. I'm not saying you shouldn't attempt it. You just need to know what's coming.

When I'm long retired and my son Macsen is all grown up and ready to take on some proper mountains with his old man, I'll have a list in my head of the climbs from my career that I'd like to revisit with him. The Portet? I know what I'll say. 'Macs, let's leave that one to next year. One day. Just not this one.'

Col du Tourmalet

There are so many reasons to remember the Tourmalet, so many ways to think about it. It's a lifelong favourite of the Tour de France in a way that other mountain passes never will be. It's different to everything else around it; it's long and spectacular and goes very, very high. It's a mountain you have to see.

Yet for me, it's about one man. Nico Portal, for seven years my sporting director at Team Sky and Ineos, but much more than that to everyone who knew him.

You couldn't help but like Nico. You met him for ten minutes and you walked away feeling happier. He should have been annoying – good-looking, talented, charismatic, French. But he wasn't. And he was incredible as a DS, and an even better man. He was the voice in my ear on every Tour de France I rode from 2013 until his sudden death, aged forty, in March 2020. Encouraging me. Advising me. Counselling me. All this while driving a car round difficult roads at remarkable speeds and in absolute safety. I told you he should have been annoying.

Nico was based in Pau, at the foothills of the Pyrenees, for a long time, before moving to Andorra with his family towards the end. And he loved those mountains, and he loved the Tourmalet most of all – as a challenge, when he was a pro rider; as an essential part of almost every Tour; as a place to be in the high mountains, and the views and air and peace they bring.

All that rubbed off on me, those elements of a climb that I wasn't naturally drawn to. So when I ride the Tourmalet now, I think of Nico, and his love for it, and how we all felt about him.

And he's right. It's a climb that doesn't get the praise and affection it deserves. We talk about Alpe d'Huez and Mont Ventoux, but the Tourmalet is the daddy of the Pyrenees. You can't become a Tour great without riding it well. It goes on for ever. It goes beyond 2100 metres, which means you get the complete climate range from bottom to top: scorching on its lower slopes, pouring bottles of water over your head; 15°C colder at the top, all fog and chill winds and shivers.

But it can get taken for granted, partly because it's the exception to have a stage actually finish up there, and it's totally different riding a climb mid-race to racing up it at the end. You ride the Tourmalet en route to another mountain, as we did at the Tour in 2018, and it's likely to be a solid pace but nothing too crazy. When it's the final climb it all goes off. One of them you're going as fast as you can, the other you're wasting as little energy as possible.

My first year at Sky we got a taste of both. The Tourmalet

during stage sixteen and then as a finish climb the next day. Back then I was carrying a little extra track weight – you call it weight, I'll call it power – so found it tougher getting uphill. My conclusion at the end of those two days? The Tourmalet during the stage was harder. You're either going all out to hang on to the peloton, or you're already dropped and trying frantically not to lose more time. Whereas on a finish climb you know, more or less, how much time you have to get within the limit for that day, so you can take it as easy as possible. I still remember the shock of watching how the leaders finished, on TV in the team bus an hour or so later – Alberto Contador and Andy Schleck going hammer and tongs through the mist. Jeez, is that the same climb I just rode up?

But that was a rare one. Usually the Tourmalet is a 'transition' climb, and so can feel like it has less of an influence on the battle for the yellow jersey than one that's always the final act on stage rather than the support. And it's how incongruous it can feel in its natural surroundings, too – a functional road that goes as straight as it can for as long as it can rather than wherever it wants, as most climbs in the Pyrenees do. Roads round here are usually shorter and steeper. They're twisty, flamboyant, things going on all over the place. They're 'sod it, let's build a road over this'.

The Alps are the sensible ones. Wide roads, regular hairpins. Towns at the top. Clean lines and sober engineering. And the Tourmalet fits that model far better than it does the Pyrenees. It's like meeting three brothers who are all short and muscular, and then finding out the fourth one, the youngest, is a foot taller. Say hello to Steve, he's different.

There isn't much wiggle-waggle with the Tourmalet. There isn't much cover. It doesn't terrify you – we won't all be in cowed silence on the team bus after the morning briefing that day – but the fact you can see so far up and down the road brings its own problems. If you're dropped on a twisty climb, you know you're dropped. You deal with it and crack on as best you can. If you're dropped on the long straights on the Tourmalet, you can see your rivals riding away from you. You can't escape the reality. It's like being dumped by a long-term partner, and then whenever you go out you bump into them at every pub or bar you go into. She's ready to move on, but you can't, because you're constantly being reminded of your own failures.

Even the ski station at La Mongie, halfway up on the western approach, has a functional Alpine feel rather than a maverick Pyrenean one. Grey concrete, tall, brutal apartment blocks. It's a place built for necessity rather than pleasure. But it's still the place you look forward to most as you climb, because here there's accommodation to be found, and so it's where support at the roadside is most dense.

Just make sure your supporters have worked out which

way up the mountain you're going. In 2016, my father-in-law and some of his mates flew out to watch me in the Tour. The day before, when Steve Cummings had won the stage that went up the Col d'Aspin, I'd met them at the finish. 'Don't worry, Ger, we've got our spot, straight outside the apartment.' 'You know we're descending that side, yeah? So you'll see us all for about three seconds as we go past at 50 miles an hour?' 'Erm . . .

And it is a fast descent, too. A long, straight road means you can get up to some real speeds, even quicker if you're slipstreaming behind a car, as a few try to do. I remember José Joaquín Rojas flying past me in 2014, tucked in behind the Movistar team car on the descent before the final climb up to Hautacam. I was going at least 80kph. They must have been at 120kph. It was genuinely frightening. He was spotted by the commissaires and booted out of the race, but still.

The climb. From the usual side, coming through Sainte Marie de Campan, it's solid. 17.2km, an average gradient of 7.4%, a jump up to 13% in the last knockings. The first time I rode it, I was distracted by the avalanche tunnels the road slides under – those open-sided things so familiar from helicopter shots on the TV coverage when I was a kid. There are no avalanche tunnels on the Tumble or Rhigos in south Wales, so they were the Tour as far as I was concerned. I may have been the only man smiling on that ascent, but it mattered to me.

By 2011, I was over the initial shock and found myself in the break going towards the summit. It was a stinker of a Tour for the team; Brad Wiggins crashed out, and we were desperate for some sort of lift. So when I dropped Jeremy Roy, the only other rider left, I decided to be sensible. We're only a kilometre from the top, better wait for him so we can ride together to the finish an hour on and have a better chance of staying away for the stage win.

It was a magnificent plan, right up to the point where he suddenly sprinted past me as we began to crest the climb. You fool, I thought. You're too far down the King of the Mountains classification for these points to make any difference to anyone. Save your legs, son, we'll need them for the hard yards ahead. It was only in the post-stage interview at the finish that I discovered there was a 5000 Euro prize for the first rider over the Tourmalet. Fool? There was only one fool on that mountain, and it was the one who'd opened his wallet and let a beaten man stick his hand in and help himself.

It was maybe tougher still in 2019, when we finished on top. I was struggling to stay with the front group and had to let them go, be sensible and work my own pace rather than try to match them, only to blow completely in the steep final kilometre. The bottom of the climb had been unpleasant, too, Andrey Amador riding hard for Movistar to spoil the Ineos party and setting a crazy pace. He was spiking: one minute brutally fast, then easing off for two minutes and going again. In the following group you loathe that sort of tactic. It just ruins everyone's day. Physically, you can handle it as much as the other guys, but mentally, it's a cruel sort of challenge. Having someone do it to you is so much worse than doing it to yourself. Knowing he's not riding for the summit, so he can do what he wants, but you are, and so the last thing you want is that sort of maverick playfulness. It planted a seed in my mind: when I'm no longer riding for the general classification in the Tour, when my role is similarly unshackled, I might ride on the Tourmalet like a right bastard, too. Just to see what it's like.

Col du Galibier

From the south (Col de Lautaret to the top, Tour de France 2019 stage eighteen)

Tim Kerrison: 'It's a high-altitude climb – the final section starting at 2000m after the long fast climb of Col de Lautaret from Briançon, and climbing up to over 2600m. You can see the effect of the altitude and the long previous climbs on the average power – "only" 360w. Despite this, G still managed a maximum power of 955w during an attack towards the top of the climb.'

Duration: 23 mins 28 secs

Distance: 8.53km

Ave speed: 21.7kph

Ave power: 360w

Ave cadence: 82

Ave heart rate: 154bpm

You save up the cash and go to the Alps, ride the big climbs, have an amazing week with your mates. You stick your bike back in the car, drive home and look forward to strolling into the office on Monday to a chorus of admiration from your friends and colleagues.

And that's what happens when you tell them you

rode up Alpe d'Huez, because they've all heard of Alpe d'Huez. And then you tell them you went up the Galibier, and Doris from accounts shrugs, and a few people start looking at their phones, and everyone gradually disperses and you want to shout at them, 'But it's the Galibier! It's horrible!'

This is the fate of the Galibier. It's a monster – 2642 metres at the summit, thirty-five kilometres long from the northern side if you include the Col du Télégraphe, as we always do. There's nothing up there but snow and pain and remorse. No towns, no villages anywhere near the top, just a tunnel that you're not allowed to cycle through anyway. You come from the southern side, via Briançon, and it might be even worse – not quite as long, but with cars flying past you, and the road disappearing up and away straight in front of you. There is nothing soft and cuddly about it. It's the sort of place where you fear bad things happen. If dragons roam anywhere, they roam on the Galibier. And if you see them, it's too late, because there's no phone signal up there and it's too far from anywhere to run away. Still shrugging, Doris?

Happier memories. In 2011, Team Sky had Rigoberto Urán in the white jersey for best young rider. While he cracked on stage eighteen, as we finished atop the Galibier, I was in the front group trying to help him out as the big GC guys went after each other – Cadel Evans running low on teammates, Andy Schleck attacking from miles out, a headwind up the long drag to the right-hand turn, so I could sit back in the wheels. As it all kicked off and Rigo cracked, I stayed with him to the line. And for the first time, I started thinking, what if I'd ridden for myself today? Used my energy for me, rather than a teammate? How far would I have got?

The next day it was the Galibier again, this time from the Télégraphe side en route to a finish up Alpe d'Huez. Still hoping for Rigo, still thrilled to be around the racing right in the guts of the yellow-jersey battle. And, as it turned out, the reason I'll always associate the Galibier with French hero Thomas Voeckler.

The whole of France was in a Tommy frenzy, as he fought for what would end up being a heroic fourth overall. I was in the same group as him for a while on the ascent of the Galibier, and he was throwing in the full set of Voeckler moves: pulling faces, sticking his tongue out, rocking his bike dramatically from side to side. It's the sort of behaviour that, had he been British, would have made him the target of much mickey-taking in the pubs and playgrounds, in the same way that Welshmen delighted in mimicking Jonny Wilkinson's distinctive pre-kick hands-clasped crouch. Since he was instead in France, they lapped it up. And so the noise for him on the Galibier was for a conquering hero rather than a climb, and I was glad of all of it, because it distracted me from the horrors I was going through alongside him.

You don't often have a summit finish on the Galibier. You do always fear it. It's so high, so bleak. On Tenerife you can do the Vilaflor climb and almost forget you're 2100m up because there are trees and soft views and warm breezes. On the Galibier there's no escape. Rocks, dirty snow, squeaking marmots and you.

And I couldn't enjoy this one from the start. Nervous, apprehensive of what was to come. A breakaway a minute up the road, Alberto Contador's teammate Chris Anker Sørensen attacking early to set alarm bells ringing. If a teammate goes, the leader might follow. And he did, just a couple of kilometres into the climb. A sudden shout on the team radio: 'Contador attack!' Hoping to blow the legs off his rivals, knowing what he was doing to our heads.

We all looked at each other with the same question on our lips: why? Why here? You're two kilometres into the Télégraphe. We can't even see the Galibier proper yet. Do us all a favour. Wait another 10km. You could still get your gap. You just won't destroy us all in the trying.

I say the southern side is worse. That's like saying I'd like to be hit by Tyson Fury's right hand rather than his left. Neither option is good. Neither is fun.

The Télégraphe side means you're doing a tough climb on top of a tough climb. You go up, drop and then climb again. That's not fair. And the Briançon side just drags. In the 2019 Tour, teammates were thin on the ground for me and Egan Bernal; Michał Kwiatkowski had gone,

Gianni Moscon had gone, Luke Rowe was long gone. Dylan van Baarle was up the road in the break. So poor old Jonathan Castroviejo had to do a massive turn on the front of our group, all the way from the bottom to the turn right with about 8km to go, and he could see Dylan's group up there ahead of us, all the way.

It was less hare in front of a greyhound than plate of food in front of a starving man. Tantalized, tortured, confused.

Castro, panting into the team radio: 'Dylan, are you sitting up?'

Dylan: 'Yeah, I'm not pushing it.'

Castro: 'So why are you so far away?'

Dylan: 'I'm going easy.'

Castro: 'Slow down! Please!'

I think back to the start, too. My very first Tour, in 2007; my first experience of the high mountains anywhere. It barely felt like I was in the Tour. My race was with myself, with the grupetto, with the time cut. Could I survive another day? Could I survive the next hour?

The Galibier came on stage nine, after the first rest day of the Tour. Stage eight had been brutal for me, dropped on a cat 2 climb 40km into the race, only rejoining the grupetto on the final climb to Tignes after 110km chasing on my own. And stage eight hadn't even had a hors-categorie climb. Stage nine had two, starting on the Iseran and then hitting the Télégraphe and Galibier. Doomsday to come, doomsday in the team meeting. Our Colombian climber, Mauricio Soler, told to go all out from the very start. Me thinking 'What? Please, no, just a few kilometres easy, please ...' Me being told 'Thomas, bocca lupo.' Good luck. Cheers.

But it worked. To me it was like an Olympic team pursuit final, albeit ninety times as long. An extra two espressos on the bus, on the start line before anyone else. If I was going to go home today, I was at least going home fighting. Spotting the green jersey of Tom Boonen, knowing he would be pacing himself up the climbs, knowing his team would give him riders to help him through. Sitting with him, with the great Tom Boonen, surviving, making it through. I even spotted my old mate Mike Davies, in his lime-green Cardiff Jif team kit halfway up the Galibier – the same man I'd ridden out with to watch the Five Valleys in South Wales six years before. The only negative was the bidon of water he handed me from the roadside. A bidon he had carried up in the blazing heat, which now had the temperature of bath water. Ideal in South Wales; maybe less so on the Galibier.

It all makes me wish there was more of a song and dance at the top when you do make it. For us pro riders, we can zip up our jerseys, take on food and get ready for the descent. For the club rider, for the tourist, you can take a photo by the sign that says, 'Col du Galibier: altitude 2642m', and that's it. Nothing else to show the unconverted, postcards to send back to the office, no tea towel to buy for Doris. Just you and the old snow and the lonely, blasted slopes.

Alpe d'Huez

19/07/2018, Tour de France stage 12
Tim Kerrison: 'G was in the yellow jersey, having won the previous stage. This was the queen stage: 175km and over 5000m of climbing. He started this final climb after more than 4½ hours of racing and 4000m of climbing.'
Duration, whole climb: 41 mins 12 secs
Distance: 13.4km
Ave speed: 19.4kph
Ave power: 385w
Ave heart rate: 156bpm

Tim Kerrison: 'Then when Vincenzo Nibali crashed and the pace in the lead group slowed, the power dropped to under 300w and HR dropped from 163 to 148 over one minute.'
First big attack: max power 922w
Second big attack: max power 1117w
'This period lasted around 5 minutes. It was very stop-start, and average power was only 332w, which allowed G to recover a bit for the final sprint.'
Final sprint (from last corner to finish line):
Duration: 14 seconds

Distance: 0.18km
Ave speed: 43.7
Peak power: 1194w
Ave heart rate: 162bpm

So you know all about Alpe d'Huez. Everyone does. It's an icon, a target, a dream. It's a t-shirt, a poster, a tattoo. You've followed the battles and counted the hairpins and maybe even been among the street-corner parties that watch it all go by.

But you don't really know Alpe d'Huez, not until you've ridden it, not until you've ridden it in the Tour.

Alpe d'Huez is all those things, but it's also a drag queen. During the day, when there's no one around and all is calm, it's a straight-laced businessman. It's neat and organized and clean. When the night comes, when the punters are in and the bar's packed and everyone's watching – then it's showtime. Out comes the flamboyance and the colour, the noise and the madness, the drama and the adventures you can never forget.

All climbs are different on a training ride rather than in a race. That's what you come to expect, as a pro rider. Training is silence, except for your breathing, and maybe the occasional topic of conversation with your teammate. Racing is giving it all meaning. Racing is hitting a switch and lighting the whole place up.

But there are transformations and then there is the

Alpe when the Tour comes calling. I've ridden up it in the Dauphine, a big stage race in its own right, a big race with big names who have lofty ambitions. I was in the green jersey. There were plenty of spectators. It was fine. It was lively.

And then I've done it in the Tour, wearing the yellow jersey, and suddenly, you can't see the road. It's all faces and flags and chaos. It's Moses parting the Red Sea, right in front of your face. It's pedalling into a thick cloud of orange smoke and sucking half of it down into your lungs. It's noise in your ear so loud it's distorting, as if you're standing next to the biggest speaker in a heaving nightclub.

The training ride is walking into the same nightclub at midday on a Saturday. It's empty and quiet. The Dauphine is strolling across the dancefloor at 7pm that evening, when the early birds are standing around with vodka-tonics. The Tour? It's 2am and the main DJ's on and everyone is wasted, and you can't tell if that bloke coming your way wants to punch you or tell you he loves you.

Because Alpe d'Huez is so famous, such a regular visitor, you can forget what it's really like. Familiarity breeds confusion. In my head, I've sometimes dismissed it as all hairpins and glamour. This is a mistake, because it's hard, and it is hard from the start. The run-in is almost boring, flying along a long, straight valley road with the wind in your sails. But it's tense, the anticipation of what is to come building with every pedal stroke. You try to take on any final solid foods, or just a few extra gels. You'll need it.

The peloton is one long line. Nobody wants to expend any more energy than necessary until the final kilometre before the climbs. Then the rush – you flick past a couple of roundabouts in Bourg-d'Oisans, and you hit it. just under fourteen kilometres at an average of just over 8%, but those first two kilometres all above 10%, and all that follows a slog – a long, relentless slog. It tails off a little at the end, but even then, it kicks up again. Alpe d'Huez never lets you go, not truly.

And so that unparalleled support makes the climb easier. It brings its dangers; you know any one of those thousands of people could have a devastating effect on the race, as that wandering fan did when he brought down Vincenzo Nibali in 2018. But that feeling of being at the front, leading the charge through the parting sea of fans, of them being so close you can smell them, let alone see or hear them – it's amazing to experience. It draws your attention away from what your legs and lungs are screaming at you. On your recon ride you always know precisely where you are and how long you've got left to suffer. Oh God, it's only hairpin number eighteen. Oh no, look at my data, I'm hurting and I'm not even putting out 400 watts.

Climbing is not pleasant, not really. It can be satisfying,

but it's rarely fun. But Alpe d'Huez can genuinely be enjoyable, partly because of the atmosphere on that day, partly for all that has come before. As a kid, it was the Alpe that I imagined myself to be racing when I was inching up Caerphilly mountain. It was the Alpe where the drama happened on the TV coverage of the Tour: Giuseppe Guerini leading the field up there in 1999, getting knocked off by a fan trying to take a photo, remounting and somehow going away again to win. It's Lance Armstrong and his look to Jan Ullrich, even if we now look at both of them in a different way. There is only one road up it and you don't do it by accident.

In short: if you only ride one climb in this book, make it Alpe d'Huez. If you only ride two climbs in the world, ride Alpe d'Huez and Mont Ventoux. But this is better than Ventoux. It has the hairpins, it has the party corners. It has more happening on the way up; it has a town at the top. It's not just a beautiful bleak mountain with slopes like a lunar crater.

It's a lovely road surface, smooth, flawless, as fast as a 10% climb can be. That makes sense; it's the family dinner service that only comes out for the most special of occasions. It's polished and buffed and lovingly cared for. It's incredible if you're Dutch, because the fans pretty much push you up, and if you're French and full of the natural panache, you'll get the same. But there's Irish corner and there's Welsh corner now, too, on hairpin number thirteen, and if you're a Cardiff boy riding up the mountain you always obsessed over, and you look up and there's a huge banner of you in national kit winning Commonwealth gold in 2014, and a load of your compatriots dancing about with dragons painted on their faces and lagers in their hands, there's no other climb in the world where you'd rather be.

But it's cruel. You can lead all day and halfway up the climb and be chewed up and spat out as if you never even featured. When your advantage starts going on Alpe d'Huez it drains away at a spectacular pace. Even if you're caught a few kilometres from the finish, you can still end up losing minutes if the front group keep racing. Any weakness you have, any doubts swirling around you – all are exposed on this mountain.

The beauty of the landscape? The Alpine meadows and the wild flowers in the grass? You notice none of this. Just the thin path of tarmac opening up in front of you.

It's not normal tarmac colour though. It's covered in blues, oranges and reds. Graffiti from adoring fans. Rider and team names written across the road, not that you can read any of it. If you're on the front of your group, the fans don't part in time for you to see that far ahead. If you're on someone's wheel, again, no chance. The further down the mountain you are, the more time you'll have to see it, but by then all the tyres from the riders, cars and motorbikes ahead have turned the road into a colourful, messy collage.

You watch Alpe d'Huez on TV and it's all picturesque shots from the helicopter and snowy peaks and vistas down the valley. You race it and they may as well be another country. Only coming back down in the team bus later that day or the next morning do you get a chance to see other mountains in the distance, the camping stoves and barbecues, the way the road snakes back on itself, chasing its own tail up the green mountainside.

And it might sound strange, but you get an even deeper appreciation for the steepness of the climb, when going down in the bus. Maybe deep in the race mentality you don't let yourself believe how steep it is. Or it's the fact that you're sat on a vehicle that's too big for these curves, rocking from side to side, higher up off the ground than you're used to, hurtling down the mountain with big drop-offs all around you. Did I just ride up that?

It suits a certain type of rider, in the Tour. If it's paced from the bottom, keeping the speed high enough to dissuade the adventurous from attacking, the diesel engines can hang in there. No great accelerations, just a relentless tempo, like the one Egan Bernal set for me and Chris Froome in 2018. If it slows down after a couple of kilometres, it's always fast at the bottom. If no one is controlling it at the front, it's a day for the pure climbers, for the mountain goats. It's steep enough that your power-to-weight ratio really comes into play. Not many big guys have won on the Alpe.

If you're suffering, it's hard not to keep looking at your power numbers. But if you can ride on feel, it's better for your head and your body. My training on the track gave me a great education in that. There have been times on a mountain stage where Froomey has congratulated me afterwards on holding the right tempo and I've told him that the power cranks stopped working halfway through the stage. He struggled to believe it, but steady and consistent is what wins Olympics medals in the 4000m of the team pursuit. And on both the track and on big climbs, it's all about not spiking. On the Alpe, an elite rider wants sustained power at around 420 or 430 watts. That's what we wanted from Egan. Had he ratcheted it up to 480 or 500, we would have had to tell him to take the edge off.

You need confidence in these calculations. If a rival team takes the pace on and starts working at 500 watts, you have to hold on to the knowledge that it's too much. You need the guts to sit up off the pace and let them go. As an experienced pro, you know that a rival can't ride at 500 watts with 8km to go and hold it. They will have to slow at some point. It's like the fast bowler who can slip one in there at 92mph but is so spent by the effort that the remaining five balls of the over are all 78mph half-volleys. So you ease back off their wheel, ride the pace that's sustainable for you and stay strong up top. Some people might say that's boring to watch, but that's how you win. You don't win by aiming at the impossible and crashing down short. Know your limits, remember your years of experience. Know your teammates, have confidence in them.

You fuel up for Alpe d'Huez before you get there. It's a forty-minute climb for us, so if you're not dehydrated at the bottom as you come through Bourg-d'Oisans, one bidon should do you. You don't want two because that's another half a kilogram you're dragging up. If your team is organized, you might be able to pick up an emergency bottle by the roadside, but you can't take a feed too close to the end of a stage, so your back-up may be a quick sip from a teammate's bottle. At 30°C in the middle of July even one mouthful of energy drink can make half a minute of difference.

Solid food? Not on the climb. You're breathing too hard. Once you're at threshold in your heart-rate zones it becomes impossible to eat. A caffeine gel at the bottom will take around twenty minutes to kick in – perfect for the critical second half of the climb. You'll feel it flare when it does. Here comes the cavalry. Or at least a lone horseman. Until then, focus on breathing, tick off hairpins, ride smooth, don't spike too much and suddenly, before you know it, you're at 4km to go.

Just don't expect to hear anything on the team radio. The earpiece might be taped on, but the noise from the sea of fans is so intense that it may as well be dangling over your shoulder. Egan did go a little too hard on a couple of occasions. I had to shout at the top of my voice just to get him to look round. Your sporting director will be barking stats and encouragement from the team car. You won't get any of it. It's just white noise – beautiful static like everything else in the baking air.

As an elite rider, you're never safe. If you can get to the open bit around 3km or so from the finish and you're still holding a lead, you might be in luck. At that point, the riders in the chase group are starting to think less about you and more about who might be the danger man in their posse. No one wants to do any unnecessary work. Looking around at each other, daring each other, playing the odds. If you're out front and your legs are still good, you can keep riding and you can stay away.

You always let someone else do the work, if you can. At 10% gradient you're working mighty hard whether you're first wheel or third, but you can mark a rival, use their tempo. In 2018, Froomey and Romain Bardet kept attacking off the front. I could sit on Tom Dumoulin and let him time-trial to the top. No one was expecting me to do anything because my Sky teammate was out there, and I was in yellow, and I was safe.

The problem is more the psychological price you pay for that. There is inflicting pain on someone else and there is having it inflicted upon you. If someone else is setting that cruel pace, you're not in control. You have no idea when this increased level of pain is going to end.

Sitting there taking it feels much worse than dancing at the front, dishing it out.

I'm not a punchy climber. I can sprint and then ease off, but I prefer to ride at my own tempo. On that baking day in 2018, I felt confident I could hold the wheel in front, whether it was Nibali or Dumoulin, and just follow. If I had to jump across to the next man up the road, I could.

But holding a fraction back can be harder than going all in. You ride at 100% and it's all you can do. You throw everything on the fire and just blaze. Ride at 95% and there's none of the mad freedom. It's almost as much pain but no longer for a finite time. It's slowly twisting the knife in your guts rather than plunging it in.

You save some power for the brain. As we approached the final few kilometres that day there was a brief, strange truce. Four of us – Froome, Bardet, Dumoulin and me – were in a line across the road, all looking at each other, all cat and mouse, all waiting for someone else to twitch first. The strangest sensation, going from 500 watts down to 200, the most prestigious stage in the world's biggest race suddenly transformed into a Sunday club ride.

I hadn't had a dig yet. I didn't have to. All the way up the mountain I hadn't thought any further ahead than the next corner. Now we were on the open section, it hit me. I'm in this. I can see the finish. I've got the legs to do it. And then I got on the right wheel, with Mikel Landa having caught us and hit the front, and I got the line right around the final corner and kept my speed and then kicked like we used to kick in our team-pursuit training on the track. Back then I was gritting my teeth giving my all just to hold the wheel of Ed Clancy; now I was kicking and gritting my teeth to win on the greatest mountain of them all. No one around me and the finish line flashing past under my wheels. You don't forget those moments. You don't forget those feelings.

I've had bad days on the Alpe, too. Racing up it twice in 2013, climbing to nearly 200m on the Col de Sarenne, descending on what had been a goat track and felt like it still was. I'd fractured the top part of my pelvis at the start of that Tour and hung on and hung on for as long as I could, and here, at last, I could hold my own and help the team. We needed everything we could get: the team car broke down on the descent, overheating from all its efforts; Chris Froome, in yellow, ran low on energy and had to take a gel from Richie Porte, both of them being fined £140 and Froomey copping a twenty-second penalty, even as he hung on to the overall race lead.

In 2015, it was the crowds. The penultimate stage of the Tour, with abuse coming in loud and nasty for anyone in a Team Sky jersey – Alpe d'Huez and Dutch corner the worst of it. Richie was riding in the front group, leading the way in single file, easy to spot, clouted on the back at one point. The team cars had eggs and beer lobbed at them. Our DS, Servais Knaven, had tears in his eyes, horrified that a few of his compatriots could do such a thing. Dutch riders from other teams were coming over to apologize.

We got through it, and the good times came, and when I'm fat and old, maybe that day in 2018 will be the first tale I tell the grandkids. Unless I let them find out on their own. 'Oh, you won up there too?' I'll take them on a ski trip, come to a stop by hairpin number fifteen, casually lean against the sign that has my name on it. 'What's that? Are we? I didn't know ...'

G's Top Ten Climbers

A couple of caveats before we begin. First off, this is a list of modern greats. To make my list, a rider has to have achieved their best results since I turned pro in 2007. I've got to have seen them first-hand. So if they retired in 2008, but were amazing from 2000 to 2004, I can't have them.

It's also not been easy. Every time I consider a fresh name and their results, I want to move them higher. I've got to give honourable mentions to a few who didn't make the top ten: Richie Porte, one of the most talented riders I've ever raced with, record-holder on most test climbs we did as a team, never quite getting the big results he deserves; Wout Poels, who on a good day is unstoppable; Rigoberto Urán, always consistent, always fast uphill; Julian Alaphilippe, MVP of the 2019 Tour, great rider, great climber. And, without further ado, in reverse order . . .

10. Cadel Evans

Thibaut Pinot was close here, but I have to get Cadel in – not the purest of climbers but a Tour winner and twice second, world champion, winner of Flèche Wallonne. He should definitely be on the list.

9. Carlos Sastre

Sastre wasn't someone who'd light up the race. But he was always there or thereabouts, and he won the Tour in 2008 and won the polka-dot jersey the same year, which is rare for a reason.

8. Joaquim Rodríguez

Proper palmares – a podium in all three Grand Tours, fourteen stage wins in those biggest races, Lombardie and Flèche. You don't win Flèche up the Mur de Huy if you can't climb. His longevity and consistency put him above Sastre in my eyes. I'd really like to put him higher, but the guys in front were just better on the bigger Tour climbs.

7. Egan Bernal

If I were to do this list in three years' time, I'm sure Egan would be higher, maybe at the very top. But seeing as he's only been professional for a few years he can't go too much higher, even though what he has done in that period is phenomenal.

6. Andy Schleck

Burst on the scene with second in the Giro in 2007, aged twenty-two; winner of the 2010 Tour; competitive in the Ardennes. From 2007 to 2011 he was one of the best around. Could he, should he have done more? Maybe. But those five years were impressive.

5. Nairo Quintana

Winner of the Giro and Vuelta, if never quite capturing the Tour, which he was heavily tipped for. Still has time though; maybe he has by the time you read this. Always there in the mountains; if he falls out of GC, you can be certain he'll be up there fighting for a mountain stage.

4. Alejandro Valverde

Not the purist of climbers when it comes to the Grand Tours – but on any climb, whether 1km long or 25km, he'll be there. I'll be honest: I've switched him between third and fourth about ten times already. Winner of the Vuelta, third in Tour and Giro. Seven podium finishes at the Worlds, champion in 2018. Flèche five times. Liège four. This is too hard.

3. Vincenzo Nibali

The fact Nibali has won all three Grand Tours puts him ahead of Valverde for me. Also, throw in some Classics.

Exciting to watch, not necessarily great to race against though. Never afraid to have a go.

2. Alberto Contador

This was a tough decision. Contador and Froomey are very different riders. Both the best of their generation. Would Contador's palmares be any different if he had Sky riding for him instead? Won all three Grand Tours, and someone you could never let off the leash; we'd always try to keep him in check. He was second in Paris-Nice when I won in 2016 – my biggest win at that point, and still one of my proudest moments, winning ahead of one of the greats.

1. Chris Froome

Four Tours, two Vueltas and a Giro. That was the deciding fact for me. He had so many battles over the years with all the riders in the top five of this list, but on the whole he came out on top. The most impressive thing for me is that unlike the others he could also time-trial, which made the difference in stage races. The best Grand Tour rider ever? It's hard to compare generations. But for me, he is.

Glossary

20/40
Twenty seconds of riding so fast you want to be sick; 40 seconds of getting ready to feel sick again

Berg
A small but steep and unpleasant hill in Belgium, the Netherlands or surrounding landscapes

Bidon
Water bottle

Big ring
The larger of the two chainrings on your bike; to go fast, get in the big ring

Bottom-to-top threshold
Your threshold is the maximum power you can hold for about an hour, and bottom to top means doing that from the foot of a climb to the summit

Cadence

The rhythm of your pedalling; the speed you're turning the pedals round

Chainring

The front part of your bike's gears; you have a big ring (see above) and a small ring (unless you're on a mountain bike or cyclo-cross bike – see below – in which case you might only have one)

Classics

The big one-day races. Can be spring Classics like Strade Bianchi, cobbled Classics like the Tour of Flanders, or Ardennes Classics like Amstel Gold Race. All thrillers, all races you want on your palmares (see below)

Crosswind

Tailwinds are lovely. Headwinds are a pain. Crosswinds split up the peloton and blow a race apart

Cyclo-cross

Races of about an hour's duration on mud, sand, gravel and through big puddles; huge fun, massive in Belgium and the Netherlands

Derailleur

How you change gears on a bike. The clever thing at the back that moves the chain from one sprocket (see below) to another

Domestique

The unsung rider who works solely for his team leaders' benefit, carrying extra bottles, letting them shelter on his or her wheel, sacrificing all their energy on the leaders' behalf. I've been one and benefited from several

Drafting

Slipstreaming. Ride behind another rider and there's less wind resistance. You go the same speed while using significantly less energy. Useful

Draggy

A climb that isn't super-steep but just goes on, and on, and on

DS

Directeur sportif, or sport director – the team's hands-on boss/tactical brain/genius driver during a race

First wheel

The leading rider in a group

Freewheel

To stop pedalling and let momentum take its turn

Garmin

Brand of cycling watch/computer. Can show all manner of useful metrics including heart-rate and power

GC
General classification – the overall leaders' competition in a big stage race

Granny gear
A gear so small – and thus so easy to pedal – that even a granny could use it to get up a steep hill

Green jersey
Worn by the rider leading the points competition, aka the most successful sprinter in the race

Grupetto
The little group – the last posse of riders in the field; usually tired, injured, ill or (in the mountains) overly muscular sprinters

Hairpin
A tight switchback bend

Half-wheel
To ride slightly ahead of the person alongside you, so that your front wheel is always half a wheel ahead of theirs (considered showing off and also impolite)

Headwind
When the wind blows directly at you, making everything harder, except going slower

Hors-categorie

A climb so steep that it is beyond the usual classification system. In the old days, signified that a car couldn't make it up. Today, signifies that a cyclist will hurt for a long time

One-day Monuments

The five biggest one-day races. Milan – San Remo, Tour of Flanders, Paris-Roubaix, Liege-Bastogne-Liege, and Il Lombardia

Palmares

The best results a rider has secured in their career (the closest I'll ever get to a CV)

Peloton

The largest pack of riders in a race

Red (into the)

Going too hard – as in the needle on a car's rev counter going too far round

Power meter

On-board computer that records and displays how hard you're working. Usually calculated in watts. Can be a Garmin (see above)

Right wheel

The best rider to follow; the correct wheel to be on

Second wheel

Riding in second place in a group

Secteur

A section of cobbles, usually on the famously cobbled Paris-Roubaix route

Spiking

Riding in short, unnecessary bursts of intense effort. Hurts your legs, makes you unpopular with fellow riders

Sprocket

A small metal wheel with teeth/cogs that hold the chain at the rear wheel

Standing start

To begin pedalling from a motionless position – best illustrated by Ed Clancy

Swanny

Soigneur, aka helper, aka dogsbody – the person who cleans your kit, gives you a massage and does every other job no one else in the team really wants to do

Team pursuit

A track discipline where four men in a line ride as fast as they can for 4000 metres, attempting to catch another four men also riding in a line as fast as they can for 4000 metres

Team pursuit quartet

The four men in a line going fast (see previous entry)

Third wheel

Third position in a pack

Tifosi

Fans, specifically those in Italy — noisy, passionate, pleasantly deranged

Time cut

How far behind the leader you're allowed to be at the end of a stage before being booted out for being too slow

Turbo trainer

Stationary indoor trainer that either replaces the rear wheel on your bike or provides resistance to it, thus allowing you to ride hard without leaving your own garage, lounge or back garden

Twenty-up chain-gang

Twenty riders cycling in a pack with each taking a short turn at the front before being replaced by the next rider; when working well, this looks like a chain moving in a stretched-out oval

White jersey

Jersey worn by leading young rider in a race

Yellow jersey

Jersey worn by rider leading the GC (see above)

Zone 3

Riding at around 70–80% of your maximum heart rate; pedalling so hard you can only get a few words out at a time; also, a commutable area to live in London, with access both to the CBD and surrounding countryside

Zwift

The premier online virtual training and racing system. Hook up your bike to your tablet or laptop and you can race other people round a number of beautifully detailed and designed routes

Acknowledgements

Thank you so much to:

Nico Portal, the man in my ear up most of these climbs. Forever in my heart.

My wife Sara, who makes it all possible and all of it worthwhile.

Beth, Eif, Rhys, Carys and Alys. Hilary, Howell and Alun. Without my family's support and dedication behind me I wouldn't have ridden up 95% of these climbs.

Tim Kerrison for his number crunching, input and training, which helped me travel up these climbs a lot quicker than I'd ever imagined.

James Morton, the nutritionist who got me to my ideal weight while still being powerful, which for me is the holy grail.

Tom Fordyce for once again dragging all the trials, trails and tribulations out of me.

Richard Milner and all his fantastic team at Quercus, plus David Luxton. It's been great getting the gang back together again.

Jay de Andrade and the team at Rocket Sports.

Darren Tudor and Alun and Bill Owen for their help with the Tumble.

Chris Gould and Dale Appleby for their help jogging my memory on the Welsh climbs.

The fans, from all countries, all over the world. You make racing these climbs so much more exciting and enjoyable. Keep the crazy outfits and screaming coming.